2014

FINANCIAL RATIOS

DAVID ACKAH

Ph.D. / M.Phil. / MSc / BSc / Dip

About The Author

David Ackah was born in the Western part of Ghana, precisely Egyambra in the Ahanta West District. He had his basic and secondary education from Egyambra Basic Education, and Esiama Secondary School.

He then obtains Diploma in Economics and Business Management from Colorado Technical University, and Community College of Southern Nevada. He again continues his education to University College of Management Studies - UCOMS to read BSc Accounting, as life goes on, he had an admission to study at Atlantic International University at Hawaii precisely Honolulu in USA and Colorado Technical University to read Master of Science (MSc) and Master of Philosophy (M.Phil.) in Economics, with his hard working, he had 3.98 GPA score after his Master of Science in Economics, with this, he again obtain an admission with automatic enrolment to study Doctor of Philosophy in Economics.

David also studies other professional course from the following institutions: Managing and Marketing Sales Association (MAMSA in Cherish England), Standard Diploma in Sales Management, Institute of Commercial Management (ICM in UK), Diploma in Marketing, and Institute of Export and Shipping Management (IESM in Ghana) Diploma in Marketing & Salesmanship

He has work with many companies like Tobinco Pharmaceutical Ltd as Marketing Manager in Takoradi, Nutraculture Indian Pharma as Country Manager in Ghana, and Pharmanova Ltd as a Regional Marketing Manager and Teaches in many Colleges, and Secondary schools. Currently He is a Lecturer in Uniworld University College, Institute of Distance Learning – KNUST and CEO of Regaro Group of Companies

DEDICATION

I dedicate this Book to God for his love throughout my traveling on schooling period. I again dedicate this book to my one only wife Mrs Makafui Ackah, a lecturer at Accra Poly.

ACKNOWLEDGEMENT

I first and foremost express my love to God for his blessings on me every day during and after the work, and also my old school lectures for the support to me.

And also to my lovely wife Makafui Ackah for her advice and support I really appreciate it.

TABLE OF CONTENTS

PREFACE

This book is designed primary to supplement the students who are reading degree course in the field of Business especially in Accounting, Managerial Accounting, Economics, and Finance.

The student is therefore enjoined to go through the worked examples very carefully to enable him/her to solve the problem in the field of business.

I wish to take his opportunity to thank all my family and all my friends as well as Mr Kingsley Kwabena Ansong and his family for their support

CHAPTER ONE
FINANCIAL PLANNING

Over view

Financial Planning is the process of meeting your life goals through the proper management of your finances. Life goals can include buying a home, saving for your child's education or planning for retirement. The financial planning process involves the following steps:

- Gathering relevant financial information
- Setting life goals
- Examining your current financial status
- Coming up with a financial strategy or plan for how you can meet your goals
- Implementing the financial plan
- Monitoring the success of the financial plan, adjusting it if necessary

CASH BUDGET

The cash budget contains an itemization of the projected sources and uses of cash in a future period. This budget is used to ascertain whether company operations and other activities will provide a sufficient amount of cash to meet projected cash requirements. If not, management must find additional funding sources.

The inputs to the cash budget come from several other budgets. The results of the cash budget are used in the financing budget, which itemizes investments, debt, and both interest income and interest expense.

The cash budget is comprised of two main areas, which are Sources of Cash and Uses of Cash. The Sources of Cash section contains the beginning cash balance, as well as cash receipts from cash sales, accounts receivable collections, and the sale of assets. The Uses of Cash section contains all planned cash expenditures, which comes from the Direct Materials Budget, Direct Labour Budget, Manufacturing Overhead Budget, and Selling and Administrative Expense budget. It may also contain line items for fixed asset purchases and dividends to shareholders.

If there are any unusually large cash balances indicated in the cash budget, these balances are dealt with in the financing budget, where suitable investments are indicated for them.

Similarly, if there are any negative balances in the cash budget, the financing budget indicates the timing and amount of any debt or equity needed to offset these balances.

Example of the Cash Budget

Here is an example of the cash budget, showing the sources and uses of cash by week:

EVERSON MANUFACTURING CASH BUDGET

	Week 1	Week 2	Week 3	Week 4
Beginning cash	$25,000	$55,000	-$24,000	-$63,000
Sources of Cash				
+ Cash sales	+10,000	+12,000	+15,000	+18,000
+ Accounts receivable collected	+180,000	+185,000	+180,000	+192,000
+ Asset sales	+30,000	0	+10,000	+25,000
= Total cash available	**$245,000**	**$252,000**	**$181,000**	**$172,000**
Uses of Cash				
- Direct materials	-$87,000	-$91,000	-$99,000	-$107,000
- Direct labor	-19,000	-20,000	-23,000	-25,000
- Manufacturing overhead	-29,000	-30,000	-34,000	-37,000
- Selling & administrative	-35,000	-35,000	-38,000	-38,000
- Asset purchases	-20,000	0	-50,000	0
- Dividend payments	0	-100,000	0	0
= Total uses of cash	**-$190,000**	**-$276,000**	**-$244,000**	**-$207,000**
Net Cash Position	**$55,000**	**-$24,000**	**-$63,000**	**-$35,000**

The example shows that an inordinately large dividend payment in the second week of the cash budget, coupled with a large asset purchase in the following week, places the company in a negative cash position. Paying out such a large dividend can be a problem for lenders, who do not like to issue loans so that companies can use the funds to pay their shareholders and thereby weaken their ability to pay back the loans. Thus, it may be wiser for the company to consider a small dividend payment and avoid a negative cash position.

OTHER CASH BUDGET ISSUES

Cash balances may fluctuate considerably within a single accounting period, thereby masking cash shortfalls that can put a company in serious jeopardy. To spot these issues, it is quite common to create and maintain cash forecasts on a weekly basis. Though these short-term budgets are reasonably accurate for perhaps a month, the precision of forecasting declines rapidly thereafter, so many companies then switch to budgeting on a monthly basis. In essence, a weekly cash budget begins to lose its relevance after one month, and is largely inaccurate after two months.

CHAPTER TWO
FINANCIAL RATIO ANALYSIS

OVER VIEW

Financial ratio analysis involves calculating certain standardized relationship between figures appearing in the financial statements and then using those relationships called ratios to analyse the business' financial position and financial performance.

Due to varying size of businesses different comparison of two businesses is not possible. Certain techniques have to be applied in simplifying the financial statements and making them comparable. These include financial ratio analysis and common-size financial statements.

IMPORTANCE OF FINANCIAL RATIO ANALYSIS

- Financial ratios are mathematical comparisons of financial statement accounts or categories. These relationships between the financial statement accounts help investors, creditors, and internal company management understand how well a business is performing and areas of needing improvement.
- Financial ratios are the most common and widespread tools used to analyze a business' financial standing. Ratios are easy to understand and simple to compute.
- They can also be used to compare different companies in different industries. Since a ratio is simply a mathematically comparison based on proportions, big and small companies can be use ratios to compare their financial information.
- In a sense, financial ratios don't take into consideration the size of a company or the industry. Ratios are just a raw computation of financial position and performance.
- Ratios allow us to compare companies across industries, big and small, to identify their strengths and weaknesses.

CATEGORIES OF FINANCIAL RATIOS

Financial ratios are often divided up into six main categories, which include the following:

Liquidity Ratios

Liquidity is the ability of a business to pay its current liabilities using its current assets. Information about liquidity of a company is relevant to its creditors, employees, banks, etc. current ratio, quick ratio, cash ratio and cash conversion cycle are key measures of liquidity.

Solvency Ratios

Solvency is a measure of the long-term financial viability of a business which means its ability to pay off its long-term obligations such as bank loans, bonds payable, etc.. Information about solvency is critical for banks, employees, owners, bond holders, institutional investors, government, etc.. Key solvency ratios are debt to equity ratio, debt to capital ratio, debt to assets ratio, times interest earned ratio, fixed charge coverage ratio, etc.

Profitability Ratios

Profitability is the ability of a business to earn profit for its owners. While liquidity ratios and solvency ratios are relationships that explain the financial position of a business profitability ratios are relationships that explain the financial performance of a business. Key profitability ratios include net profit margin, gross profit margin, operating profit margin, return on assets, return on capital, return on equity, etc.

Activity ratios

Activity ratios explain the level of efficiency of a business. Key activity ratios include inventory turnover, days sales in inventory, accounts receivable turnover, days sales in receivables, etc.

Performance ratios

Performance ratios include cash flows to revenue ratio, cash flows per share ratio, cash return on assets, etc. and they aim at determining the quality of earnings.

Coverage Ratios

Coverage ratios are supplementary to solvency and liquidity ratios and measure the risk inherent in lending to the business in long-term. They include debt coverage ratio, interest coverage ratio (also known as times interest earned), reinvestment ratio, etc

Financial ratio analysis is a useful tool for users of financial statement. It has following advantages:

Advantages

1. It simplifies the financial statements.
2. It helps in comparing companies of different size with each other.
3. It helps in trend analysis which involves comparing a single company over a period.
4. It highlights important information in simple form quickly. A user can judge a company by just looking at few numbers instead of reading the whole financial statements.

Limitations

Despite usefulness, financial ratio analysis has some disadvantages. Some key demerits of financial ratio analysis are:

1. Different companies operate in different industries each having different environmental conditions such as regulation, market structure, etc. Such factors are so significant that a comparison of two companies from different industries might be misleading.
2. Financial accounting information is affected by estimates and assumptions. Accounting standards allow different accounting policies, which impairs comparability and hence ratio analysis is less useful in such situations.

3. Ratio analysis explains relationships between past information while users are more concerned about current and future information.

FORMULA AND CALCULATION
ASSET TURNOVER RATIOS

Asset turnover ratio is the ratio of a company's sales to its assets. It is an efficiency ratio which tells how successfully the company is using its assets to generate revenue.

There are a number of variants of the ratio like total asset turnover ratio, fixed asset turnover ratio and working capital turnover ratio. In all cases the numerator is the same i.e. net sales (both cash and credit) but denominator is average total assets, average fixed assets and average working capital respectively.

Formula

Following formulas are used to calculate each of the asset turnover ratios:

$$\text{Total Asset Turnover Ratio} = \frac{\text{Net Sales}}{\text{Average Total Assets}}$$

$$\text{Fixed Asset Turnover Ratio} = \frac{\text{Net Sales}}{\text{Average Fixed Assets}}$$

$$\text{Working Capital Turnover Ratio} = \frac{\text{Net Sales}}{\text{Average Net Working Capital}}$$

Analysis

If a company can generate more sales with fewer assets it has a higher turnover ratio which tells it is a good company because it is using its assets efficiently. A lower turnover ratio tells that the company is not using its assets optimally. Total asset turnover ratio is a key driver of return on equity as discussed in the DuPont analysis.

Example

As at 1 January 2011 Gamma had total assets of $100, total fixed assets of $60 and net working capital of $20. During FY 2011 it generated sales of $200 with COGS of $160 and its total assets as at 30 December 2011 were $120. During the year it charged depreciation of $10 and there were no fixed asset additions during the year. Current assets and current liabilities were $50 and $30 as at the year end. Calculate total asset turnover, fixed asset turnover and working capital turnover ratios.

Solution

Average total assets = (100+120)/2

= $110

Sales are $200 so total asset turnover is $200/$110 = 1.82.

If the industry average total asset turnover ratio is 1.2 we can conclude that the company has used its asset more effectively in generating revenue.

Opening fixed assets were $60, closing fixed assets are $60-$10=$50.

Average fixed assets are hence ($60+$50)/2=$55. This gives us fixed asset turnover of $200/$55 = 3.63

Opening working capital is $20, closing working capital is $20 ($50-$30); this gives us average working capital of $20 and resulting working capital turnover ratio of $200/$20=10. Asset turnover ratio should be looked at together with the company's financing mix and its profit margin for a better analysis as discussed in DuPont analysis.

CASH CONVERSION CYCLE

Cash conversion cycle is the time it takes a company to convert its resource inputs into cash. It measures how effectively a company is managing its working capital.

Formula

$$\text{Cash Conversion Cycle} = \text{DSO} + \text{DIO} - \text{DPO}$$

Where DSO is days sales outstanding, DIO is days inventory outstanding and DPO is days payables outstanding.

It can also be calculated if we already know the operating cycle:

$$\text{Cash Conversion Cycle} = \text{Operating Cycle} - \text{Days Payables Outstanding}$$

Analysis

Shorter the cash conversion cycle the better the company is off because it has to lock up cash for a relatively smaller period of time.

Example

Company K has receivables turnover ratio of 12, inventory turnover ratio of 10 and payable turnover ratio of 8. Find the cash conversion cycle.

Solution

We first need to convert the turnover measures to number of days measures.

Days sales outstanding = 365/receivables turnover ratio

= 365/12

= 30.42 days

Days inventory outstanding = 365/inventory turnover ratio

= 365/10

= 36.4 days

Days payables outstanding = 365/payables turnover ratio

= 365/8

= 45.63 days

Cash conversion cycle = DSO + DIO − DPO

= 30.42 + 36.4 − 45.63

= 21.19

If the industry average cash conversion ratio is 25 the company is better off than other companies.

CASH RATIO

Cash ratio is the ratio of cash and cash equivalents of a company to its current liabilities. It is an extreme liquidity ratio since only cash and cash equivalents are compared with the current liabilities. It measures the ability of a business to repay its current liabilities by only using its cash and cash equivalents and nothing else.

Formula

Cash ratio is calculated using the following formula:

$$\text{Cash Ratio} = \frac{\text{Cash} + \text{Cash Equivalents}}{\text{Current Liabilities}}$$

Cash equivalents are assets which can be converted into cash quickly whereas current liabilities are those liabilities which are to be settled within 12 months or the business cycle.

Interpretation

A cash ratio of 1.00 and above means that the business will be able to pay all its current liabilities in immediate short term. Therefore, creditors usually prefer high cash ratio. But businesses usually do not plan to keep their cash and cash equivalent at level with their current liabilities because they can use a portion of idle cash to generate profits. This means that a normal value of cash ratio is somewhere below 1.00.

Example 1:

A company has following assets and liabilities at the year ended December 31, 2009:

Cash	$34,390
Marketable Securities	12,000
Accounts Receivable	56,200
Prepaid Insurance	9,000
Total Current Liabilities	73,780

Calculate cash ratio from the above information:

Solution

Cash ratio = (34,390 + 12,000) / 46,390
= 102,590 / 73,780
= 0.63

Example 2:

Calculate cash ratio from the following information.

Cash	$21,720
Treasury Bills	18,500
Accounts Receivable	35,930

Total Current Liabilities	82,960

Solution
Since treasury bills are marketable securities thus we will calculate cash ratio as follows:
Quick ratio = (21,720 + 18,500) / 82,960
$\qquad$ = 40,220 / 82,960
$\qquad$ = 0.48

CURRENT RATIO

Current ratio is the ratio of current assets of a business to its current liabilities. It is the most widely used test of liquidity of a business and measures the ability of a business to repay its debts over the period of next 12 months.

Formula
Current ratio is calculated using the following formula:

$$\text{Current Ratio} = \frac{\text{Current Assets}}{\text{Current Liabilities}}$$

Both the above figures can be obtained from the balance sheet of the business. Current assets are the assets of a business expected to be converted to cash or used up in next 12 months or within the normal operating cycle of the business. Current liabilities on the other hand are the obligations of a business which need to be settled within next 12 months or within the normal operating cycle.

Analysis
Current ratio matches current assets with current liabilities and tells us whether the current assets are enough to settle current liabilities. Current ratio below 1 shows critical liquidity problems because it means that total current liabilities exceed total current assets. General rule is that higher the current ratio better it is but there is a limit to this. Abnormally high value of current ratio may indicate existence of idle or underutilized resources in the company.

Examples
Example 1: On December 31, 2009 Company A had current assets of $100,000 and current liabilities of $50,000. Calculate its current ratio.

Solution
Current ratio = $100,000 ÷ $50,000 = 2.00

Example 2: On December 31, 2010 Company B had total asset of $150,000, equity of $75,000, non-current assets of $50,000 and non-current liabilities of $50,000. Calculate the current ratio.

Solution

To calculate current ratio, we need to calculate current assets and current liabilities first:

Current Assets = Total Asset − Non-Current Assets

$\qquad$ = \$150,000 − \$50,000

$\qquad$ = \$100,000

Total Liabilities = Total Assets − Total Equity

$\qquad$ = \$150,000 − \$75,000

$\qquad$ = \$75,000

Current Liabilities = \$75,000 − \$50,000

$\qquad$ = \$25,000

Current Ratio = \$100,000 ÷ \$25,000 = 4.00

DAYS' INVENTORY ON HAND RATIO

Days' inventory on hand (also called days' sales in inventory or simply days of inventory) is an accounting ratio which measures the number of days a company takes to sell its average balance of inventory. It is also an estimate of the number of days for which the average balance of inventory will be sufficient. Days' sales in inventory ratio are very similar to inventory turnover ratio and both measure the efficiency of a business in managing its inventory.

Formula

Days' inventory on hand is usually calculated by dividing the number of days in a period by inventory turnover ratio for the period as shown in the following formula:

$$\text{Days of Inventory} = \frac{\text{Number of Days in the Period}}{\text{Inventory Turnover for the Period}}$$

Thus, if we have inventory turnover ratio for the year, we can calculate days' inventory on hand by dividing number of days in a year i.e. 365 by inventory turnover.

If we substitute inventory turnover as "cost of goods sold ÷ average inventory" in the above formula and simplify the equation, we get:

$$\text{Days of Inventory} = \frac{\text{Average Inventory}}{\text{Cost of Goods Sold}} \times \text{Number of Days in the Period}$$

Analysis

Since inventory carrying costs take significant investment, a business must try to reduce the level of inventory. Lower level of inventory will result in lower days' inventory on hand ratio. Therefore lower values of this ratio are generally favourable and higher values are unfavourable.

However, inventory must be kept at safe level so that no sales are lost due to stock-outs. Thus low value of days of inventory ratio of a company which finds it difficult to satisfy demand is not favourable.

Days' sales in inventory vary significantly between different industries. For example, business which sells perishable goods such as fruits and vegetables have very low values of days' sales in inventory whereas companies selling non-perishable goods such as cars have high values of days of inventory.

Examples

Example 1: Company Y has inventory turnover ratio of 13.5 for the year. Calculate its days' inventory on hand ratio.

Solution

Number of days in the period = 365

Days' Inventory on Hand = $365 \div 13.5 \approx 27$

Example 2: Calculate the days' sales in inventory ratio using the information given below:

Beginning Inventory	$213,000
Ending Inventory	$265,000
Cost of Goods Sold (for the quarter)	$5,712,000

Solution

Number of Days in the Period = $365.25/4 \approx 91$

Average Inventory = $(213,000 + 265,000) \div 2$
$$= \$239,000$$

Days' Sales in Inventory = $239,000 \div 5,712,000 \times 91$
$$\approx 3.8 \text{ days}$$

DAYS PAYABLES OUTSTANDING

Day's payables outstanding (DPO) is the average number of days in which a company pays its suppliers. It is also called number of days of payables.

In general, a low DPO highlights good working capital management because the company is availing early payment discounts. However, the DPO should be corroborated by other ratios, particularly the liquidity ratios. When a company's liquidity position is good, high day's payables outstanding most likely tells that the company is delaying payments to its creditors till the last possible date to shorten its cash conversion cycle. It highlights good working capital management. However, if the liquidity situation of the company is not good, a high DPO suggests that the company is facing problems paying its suppliers.

Formula

$$\text{Days Payables Outstanding} = \frac{\text{Number of Days in a Period}}{\text{Payables Turnover for the Period}}$$

Since, Payables Turnover $= \dfrac{\text{Purchases}}{\text{Average Trade Payables}}$

Days Payables Outstanding $= \dfrac{\text{Number of Days in a Period}}{\text{Purchases}} \times \text{Average Trade Payables}$

If the period is a year:

Days Payables Outstanding for a Year $= \dfrac{365}{\text{Annual Purchases}} \times \text{average trade payables}$

If figure for purchases is not available, it is calculated as:

Purchases = Cost of Goods Sold + Closing Inventory − Opening Inventory

In some situations where opening and closing inventories are immaterial, cost of goods sold can be used instead of purchases.

Example

Calculate days payables outstanding for Company A and Company B using the information given below and tell what it tells about the companies.

	Company A	Company B
Inventories at 1 January 2013	$200,000	
Inventories at 31 December 2013	100,000	
Cost of goods sold	4,000,000	
Purchases		$2,000,000
Accounts payable at 1 January 2013	250,000	250,000
Accounts payable at 31 December 2013	400,000	400,000
Current ratio	2.00	0.50
Quick ratio	1.00	0.30

Solution

Purchases of Company A = COGS + Closing Inventories − Opening Inventories

$\qquad = \$4,000,000 + \$100,000 - \$200,000$

$\qquad = \$3,900,000$

Average accounts payable for Company A = $325,000

Days payables outstanding for Company A= 365/$3,900,000*$325,000

17

$$= 30.4$$

Days payables outstanding for Company B = 365/$2,000,000*$350,000

$$= 63.8$$

Company A has good working capital management because it is paying off its creditors at the end of credit period to avoid default and at the same time shorten its conversion cycle.

Very high day's payables outstanding for Company B are not a good sign when we look at it in the context of its liquidity problems. A days payables outstanding of 63.8, current ratio of 0.5 and quick ratio of 0.3 suggest that company B is facing problems in paying its suppliers.

DAYS' SALES OUTSTANDING (DSO) RATIO

Days' sales outstanding ratio (also called average collection period or days' sales in receivables) is used to measure the average number of days a business takes to collect its trade receivables after they have been created. It is an activity ratio and gives information about the efficiency of sales collection activities.

Formula

Days Sales Outstanding is calculated using following formula:

$$DSO = \frac{Accounts\ Receivable}{Credit\ Sales} \times Number\ of\ Days$$

If possible, use the average accounts receivable during the period. Another formula which uses the accounts receivable turnover is:

$$DSO = \frac{Number\ of\ Days\ in\ the\ Period}{Accounts\ Receivable\ Turnover}$$

Analysis

Since it is profitable to convert sales into cash quickly, which means that a lower value of Days Sales Outstanding is favourable whereas a higher value is unfavourable? However it is more meaningful to create monthly or weekly trend of DSO. Any significant increase in the trend is unfavourable and indicates inefficiency in credit sales collection.

Examples

Example 1: Calculate the Days Sales Outstanding from the following information:
Net Credit Sales during the month: $644,790
Average Accounts Receivable during the month: $43,300.
Calculate the receivables turnover ratio.

Solution

Days Sales Outstanding = ($43,300 / $644,790) × 30 days = 2.01

Example 2: Following is the trend of DSO for B Company for past 6 months:

Month	DSO
01	3.10
02	3.13
03	3.48
04	3.95
05	4.16
06	5.31

Question is the average collection period for β Company improving or deteriorating?

Answer

The average collection period has a deteriorating trend.

DEBT RATIO

Debt-to-assets ratio or simply debt ratio is the ratio of total liabilities of a business to its total assets. It is a solvency ratio and it measures the portion of the assets of a business which are financed through debt.

Formula

The formula to calculate the debt ratio is:

$$\text{Debt Ratio} = \frac{\text{Total Liabilities}}{\text{Total Assets}}$$

Total liabilities include both the current and non-current liabilities.

Analysis

Debt ratio ranges from 0.00 to 1.00. Lower value of debt ratio is favourable and a higher value indicates that higher portion of company's assets are claimed by its creditors which means higher risk in operation since the business would find it difficult to obtain loans for new projects. Debt ratio of 0.5 means that half of the company's assets are financed through debts.

Examples

In order to calculate debt ratio from the balance sheet, divide total liabilities by total assets, for example:

Example 1: Total liabilities of a company are $267,330 and total assets are $680,400. Calculate debt ratio.

Solution

Debt ratio = $267,330/$680,400
= 0.393 or 39.3%

Example 2: Current liabilities are $34,600; Non-current liabilities are $200,000; and Total assets are $504,100. Calculate debt ratio.

Solution
Since total liabilities are equal to sum of current and non-current liabilities therefore,
Debt Ratio = ($34,600 + $200,000) / $504,100
= 0.465 or 46.5%.

DEBT-TO-CAPITAL RATIO

Debt-to-capital ratio is a solvency ratio that measures the proportion of interest-bearing debt to the sum of interest-bearing debt and shareholders' equity.

Interest-bearing debt includes bonds payable, bank loans, notes payable, etc. Non-interest bearing debt includes trade payable, accrued expenses, etc.

The debt-to-capital ratio is a refinement of the debt-to-assets ratio. It measures how much of the capital employed (i.e. the resources on which the company pays a cost) is debt. Higher debt included in the capital employed means higher risk of insolvency.

Formula

$$\text{Debt-to-Capital Ratio} = \frac{\text{Interest-bearing Debt}}{\text{Interest-bearing Debt} + \text{Shareholders' Equity}}$$

Example
Calculate debt-to-capital and debt-to-assets ratios for Intel Corporation (NYSE: INTC). Relevant information for the company for financial year 2012 is as follows:

	USD in million
Short-term debt	312
Accounts payable	3,023
Accrued expenses	2,972
Accrued advertising	1,015
Deferred income	1,932
Other accrued liabilities	3,644
Long-term debt	13,136
Long-term deferred tax liabilities	3,412
Other long-term liabilities	3,702
Total liabilities	**33,148**
Total shareholders' equity	**51,203**
Total assets	**84,351**

Solution

Of all the liabilities listed on the INTC balance sheet, short-term debt and long-term debt are interest-based. The rest are non-interest. Hence, they are excluded from calculation of debt-to-capital ratio.

	USD in million
Short-term debt	312
Long-term debt	13,136
Total interest-bearing debt	13,448
Total shareholders' equity	51,203
Capital employed (interest-based debt + equity)	64,651
Total liabilities	33,148
Total assets	84,351

DEBT-TO-EQUITY RATIO

Debt-to-Equity ratio is the ratio of total liabilities of a business to its shareholders' equity. It is a leverage ratio and it measures the degree to which the assets of the business are financed by the debts and the shareholders' equity of a business.

Formula

Debt-to-equity ratio is calculated using the following formula:

$$\text{Debt-to-Equity Ratio} = \frac{\text{Total Liabilities}}{\text{Shareholders' Equity}}$$

Both total liabilities and shareholders' equity figures in the above formula can be obtained from the balance sheet of a business. A variation of the above formula uses only the interest bearing long-term liabilities in the numerator.

Analysis

Lower values of debt-to-equity ratio are favourable indicating less risk. Higher debt-to-equity ratio is unfavourable because it means that the business relies more on external lenders thus it is at higher risk, especially at higher interest rates. A debt-to-equity ratio of 1.00 means that half of the assets of a business are financed by debts and half by shareholders' equity. A value higher than 1.00 means that more assets are financed by debt that those financed by money of shareholders' and vice versa.

An increasing trend in of debt-to-equity ratio is also alarming because it means that the percentage of assets of a business which are financed by the debts is increasing.

Example

Calculate debt-to-equity ratio of a business which has total liabilities of $3,423,000 and shareholders' equity of $5,493,000.

Solution

Debt-to-Equity Ratio = $3,423,000 / $5,493,000

$$\approx 0.62$$

DEFENSIVE INTERVAL RATIO

Defensive interval ratio is a liquidity ratio that measures the number of days for which the company's current quick assets can finance its daily cash expenditures assuming it is not expected to receive any cash inflows during the period. It is calculated by dividing quick assets by daily cash expenses.

A defensive interval ratio that is lower relative to industry average or to previous year's average raises alarm about liquidity problems unless there are sufficient expected cash inflows over the period

Formula

$$\text{Defensive Interval Ratio} = \frac{\text{Quick Assets}}{\text{Daily Cash Expenses}}$$

Quick Assets = Cash + Marketable Securities + Receivables

Example

The following table summarizes information about three companies. Find their defensive interval ratio and tell which company is most likely to face serious liquidity problems. (All amounts are in million dollars.)

	A	B	C
Cash	20	30	50
Marketable securities	50	25	100
Receivables	300	30	90
Prepayments	0	20	100
Inventories	0	130	300
Daily cash expenses	6	2	6
Daily cash inflows expected for next 2 months	30	2	1

Analyze the ratio assuming that the industry average defensive interval is 2 months.

Solution

	A	B	C
Cash	20	30	50
Marketable securities	50	25	100
Receivables	300	30	90
Quick assets (A)	370	85	240
Daily cash expenses (B)	6	2	6
Defensive interval (A/B)	61.7	42.5	40.0
Daily cash inflows expected for next 2 months	30	2	1

Company A's defensive interval is as much as industry average, so the company is just fine in the short-run.

Though Company B's defensive interval ratio is lower than the industry average, the company is expected to generate as much cash inflows as its cash outflows. Hence, it means it is not expected to face any significant liquidity problems.

Company C is expected to face problems because not only its defensive interval ratio is significantly lower than the industry, it's expected daily cash inflows over the period are much lower than its daily expected cash outflows. The company should either accelerate its cash inflows or arrange short-term borrowing.

DIVIDEND PAY-OUT RATIO

Dividend pay-out ratio is the ratio of dividend per share divided by earnings per share. It is a measure of how much earnings a company is paying out to its shareholders as compared to how much it is retaining for reinvestment.

Formula

$$\text{Dividend Payout Ratio} = \frac{\text{Dividend per Share}}{\text{Earnings per Share}}$$

Dividend payout ratio can also be calculated as total dividends divided by net income.

Analysis

A shareholder has two sources of return, namely periodic income in the form of dividends and capital appreciation. Dividend payout ratio tells what percentage of total earnings the company is paying back to shareholders. A healthy dividend payout ratio leads to investor confidence in the company.

Plowback ratio (also called retention rate) is equals $1 -$ payout ratio and it equals the earnings retained divided by total earnings for the period.

Example

Zeta Ltd. earned an EPS of $2 in FY 2011 when it paid $1 per share as dividends. Find its dividend payout ratio.

DIVIDEND YIELD RATIO

Dividend yield is the ratio of dividend per share to current share price. It is a measure of what percentage an investor is earning in the form of dividends.

Formula

$$\text{Dividend Yield} = \frac{\text{Dividend per Share}}{\text{Current Share Price}}$$

Dividend yield = dividend per share/current Share Price

Analysis

Dividend yield is a measure of investor return. While dividend payout ratio judges the amount of dividend in relation to the company's earnings for the period, dividend yield ratio provides a comparison of amount of dividend in relation to investment needed to purchase its share.

A company might be paying out 50% of its earnings but if the company's current share price is too high the investors might not be attracted by even the high payout ratio. A high share price will lead to low dividend yield and vice versa.

Example

Company M has an EPS of $4 in FY 2011, its dividend payout ratio is 50% and its share price is $20. Calculate the dividend yield.

Solution

Dividend per Share = EPS × Dividend Payout Ratio
$$= \$4 \times 0.5 = \$2$$
Dividend Yield = $2/$20 = 10%

If the average dividend yield in the market is 15%, investors will be less likely interested in the company's share price.

DUPONT ANALYSIS

DuPont analysis is an extended analysis of a company's return on equity. It concludes that a company can earn a high return on equity if:

- It earns a high net profit margin;
- It uses its assets effectively to generate more sales; and/or
- It has a high financial leverage

Formula

According to DuPont analysis:

Return on Equity = Net Profit Margin × Asset Turnover × Financial Leverage

$$\text{Return on Equity} = \frac{\text{Net Income}}{\text{Sales}} \times \frac{\text{Sales}}{\text{Total Assets}} \times \frac{\text{Total Assets}}{\text{Total Equity}}$$

Analysis

DuPont equation provides a broader picture of the return the company is earning on its equity. It tells where a company's strength lies and where there is a room for improvement. DuPont equation could be further extended by breaking up net profit margin into EBIT margin, tax burden and interest burden. This five-factor analysis provides an even deeper insight.

ROE = EBIT Margin × Interest Burden × Tax Burden × Asset Turnover × Financial Leverage

$$\text{Return on Equity} = \frac{\text{EBIT}}{\text{Sales}} \times \frac{\text{EBT}}{\text{EBIT}} \times \frac{\text{Net Income}}{\text{EBT}} \times \frac{\text{Sales}}{\text{Total Assets}} \times \frac{\text{Total Assets}}{\text{Total Equity}}$$

Example: Three-factor Analysis

Company A and B operate in the same market and are of the same size. Both earn a return of 15% on equity. The following table shows their respective net profit margin, asset turnover and financial leverage.

	Company A	Company B
Net Profit Margin	10%	10%
Asset Turnover	1	1.5
Financial Leverage	1.5	1

Although both the companies have a return on equity of 15% their underlying strengths and weaknesses are quite opposite. Company B is better than company A in using its assets to generate revenues but it is unable to capitalize this advantage into higher return on equity due to its lower financial leverage. Company A can improve by using its total assets more effectively in generating sales and company B can improve by raising some debt.

FIXED ASSETS TURNOVER RATIO

Fixed assets turnover ratio is an activity ratio that measures how successfully a company is utilizing its fixed assets in generating revenue. It calculates the dollars of revenue earned per one dollar of investment in fixed assets.

A higher fixed asset turnover ratio is generally better. However, there might be situations when a high fixed asset turnover ratio might not necessarily mean efficient use of fixed assets as explained in the example.

Formula

$$\text{Fixed Assets Turnover Ratio} = \frac{\text{Net Revenue}}{\text{Average Fixed Assets}}$$

Net Revenue = Gross Revenue − sales returns

$$\text{Average Fixed Assets} = \frac{\text{Opening Balance of Fixed Assets} + \text{Ending Balance of Fixed Assets}}{2}$$

Example

The following table outlines information required to calculate fixed assets turnover for Facebook, Inc. (NYSE: FB), Linkedin Corporation (NYSE: LNKD) and Wal-mart Stores Inc. (NYSE: WMT). All amounts are in million dollars.

	FB	LNKD	WMT
Net revenue	5,089	972	469,162
Fixed asset at the start of most recent year	1,475	115	112,324
Fixed asset at the end of the most recent year	2,391	187	116,681

Calculate and interpret their fixed assets turnover ratio.

Solution

$$\text{Fixed assets turnover ratio of FB} = \frac{5,089}{(1,475 + 2,391) \div 2} = 2.63$$

$$\text{Fixed assets turnover ratio of LNKD} = \frac{972}{(115 + 187) \div 2} = 6.44$$

$$\text{Fixed assets turnover of WMT} = \frac{469,162}{(112,324 + 116,681) \div 2} = 4.06$$

The figures tell that LinkedIn Corporation has most efficiently used its fixed assets. It generated $6.44 of revenue per $1 dollar of its net fixed assets over the year. Facebook, Inc. on the other hand, generated a fixed asset turnover ratio of 2.63, which means $2.63 of revenue per $1 of investment in fixed assets. LinkedIn and Facebook are competitors with almost the same age; hence the comparison using fixed asset turnover ratio is very relevant. LinkedIn appears to be the clear winner on this parameter.

Comparison between Facebook and Walmart on fixed asset turnover ratio might not be very useful because they belong to different industries and they have different age. Wal-Mart's higher fixed asset turnover ratio might be due to old age (and hence lower book value) of Wal-Mart's assets. Lower book value of fixed assets means smaller denominator in the ratio and hence higher fixed asset turnover ratio. There might be difference in capital intensity requirements of the industry.

FIXED CHARGE COVERAGE

Fixed charge coverage is a solvency ratio that measures whether earnings before interest, taxes and lease payments are sufficient to cover the interest and lease payments. It is calculated by dividing the sum of earnings before interest and taxes and lease payments by the sum of interest payments and lease payments.

Fixed charge coverage ratio is very similar to interest coverage ratio. The only difference is that fixed charge coverage ratio takes into account the annual obligations on account of lease payments too (in addition to interest payments).

The higher the ratio, the better is the solvency situation of the company. The ratio is best used together with other solvency ratios such debt ratio, financial leverage ratio, etc.

Formula

$$\text{Fixed Charge Coverage} = \frac{\text{EBIT + Lease Payments other than Interest Portion}}{\text{Interest Payments + Lease Payments}}$$

Example

Nile Inc. has the following figures for financial year ended 31 December 2012. Calculate the interest coverage and fixed coverage ratio using interest and lease payments.

	USD in million
EBT	500
Interest expense (including interest expense on capital lease obligation)	70
EBIT	570
Interest income	12
Interest payments (related to other than capital leases)	55
Operating lease rentals paid	40
Capital lease rentals paid (hint: both principal and interest)	50
Interest on capital lease included in payments	10

Solution

Lease payments = $40 million + $50 million
= $90 million

Interest payments plus lease payments = $55 million + $90 million
= $145 million

Fixed charge coverage = ($570 million + $90 million) ÷ $145 million
= 4.55

Please note that interest income is not taken into account because gross interest payments are relevant.

The lease payments added back above include the interest expense paid on capital lease obligations. The whole interest expense including the portion related to capital lease is already included in the EBIT. Adding it again by not subtracting it from lease payments, overstates the numerator by double-counting interest expense on capital leases.

A more refined calculation is given below:

Lease payments excluding interest on capital leases = $90 million − $10 million
= $80 million

Fixed charge coverage = ($570 million + $80 million) ÷ $145 million
= 4.48

Since the difference is minor, you can ignore this minor adjustment.

GROSS MARGIN RATIO

Gross margin ratio is the ratio of gross profit of a business to its revenue. It is a profitability ratio measuring what proportion of revenue is converted into gross profit (i.e. revenue less cost of goods sold).

Formula

Gross margin is calculated as follows:

$$\text{Gross Margin} = \frac{\text{Gross Profit}}{\text{Revenue}}$$

Gross profit and revenue figures are obtained from the income statement of a business. Alternatively, gross profit can be calculated by subtracting cost of goods sold from revenue. Thus gross margin formula may be restated as:

$$\text{Gross Margin} = \frac{\text{Revenue} - \text{Cost of Goods Sold}}{\text{Revenue}}$$

Analysis

Gross margin ratio measures profitability. Higher values indicate that more cents are earned per dollar of revenue which is favourable because more profit will be available to cover non-production costs. But gross margin ratio analysis may mean different things for different kinds of businesses. For example, in case of a large manufacturer, gross margin measures the efficiency of production process. For small retailers it gives an impression of pricing strategy of the business. In this case higher gross margin ratio means that the retailer charges higher mark-up on goods sold.

Examples

Example 1: For the month ended March 31, 2011, Company X earned revenue of $744,200 by selling goods costing $503,890. Calculate the gross margin ratio of the company.

Solution

Gross margin ratio = ($744,200 − $503,890) / $744,200

≈ 0.32 or 32%

Example 2:

Calculate gross margin ratio of a company whose cost of goods sold and gross profit for the period are $8,754,000 and $2,423,000 respectively.

Solution

Since the revenue figure is not provided, we need to calculate it first:

Revenue = Gross Profit + Cost of Goods Sold

Revenue = $8,754,000 + $2,423,000

Revenue = $11,177,000

Gross Margin Ratio = $2,423,000 / $11,177,000

≈ 0.22 or 22%

INVENTORY TURNOVER RATIO

Inventory turnover is the ratio of cost of goods sold by a business to its average inventory during a given accounting period. It is an activity ratio measuring the number of times per period; a business sells and replaces its entire batch of inventory again.

Formula

Inventory turnover ratio is calculated using the following formula:

$$\text{Inventory Turnover} = \frac{\text{Cost of Goods Sold}}{\text{Average Inventory}}$$

Cost of goods sold figure is obtained from the income statement of a business whereas average inventory is calculated as the sum of the inventory at the beginning and at the end of the period divided by 2. The values of beginning and ending inventory are obtained from the balance sheets at the start and at the end of the accounting period.

Analysis
Inventory turnover ratio is used to measure the inventory management efficiency of a business. In general, a higher value of inventory turnover indicates better performance and lower value means inefficiency in controlling inventory levels. A lower inventory turnover ratio may be an indication of over-stocking which may pose risk of obsolescence and increased inventory holding costs. However, a very high value of this ratio may be accompanied by loss of sales due to inventory shortage.
Inventory turnover is different for different industries. Businesses which trade perishable goods have very higher turnover compared to those dealing in durables. Hence a comparison would only be fair if made between businesses of same industry.

Examples
Example 1: During the year ended December 31, 2010, Loud Corporation sold goods costing $324,000. Its average stock of goods during the same period was $23,432. Calculate the company's inventory turnover ratio.

Solution
Inventory Turnover Ratio = $324,000 ÷ $23,432 ≈ 13.83

Example 2: Cost of goods sold of a retail business during a year was $84,270 and its inventory at the beginning and at the ending of the year was $9,865 and $11,650 respectively. Calculate the inventory turnover ratio of the business from the given information.

Solution
Average Inventory = ($9,865 + $11,650) ÷ 2 = $10,757.5
Inventory Turnover = $84,270 ÷ $10,757.5 ≈ 7.83

MARKET DEBT RATIO
Market debt ratio is a solvency ratio that measures the proportion of the book value of a company's debt to sum of the book of value of its debt and the market value of its equity. Market debt ratio is a modification of the traditional debt ratio, which is the proportion of the book value of debt to sum of the book values of debt and equity of the company.
Market debt ratio measures the level of debt of a company relative to the current market value of the company and is potentially a better measure of solvency because market values are more relevant than book values.

Formula

$$\text{Market Debt Ratio} = \frac{\text{Total Liabilities}}{\text{Total Liabilities} + \text{Market Value of Equity}}$$

Market Value of Equity = Current Share Price × Number of Shares Outstanding

Number of Shares Outstanding = Total Number of Shares Issued − Treasury Shares

For companies with debt that trades in secondary markets, including the market value of debt can further refine the market debt ratio.

Example

Calculate the market debt ratio for McGraw Hill Financial Inc. (NYSE: MGHF) using the following data from 31 December 2012 and compare it with the debt ratio for the same period.

Total Liabilities (USD In million)	5,475
Total shareholders' equity (USD in million)	767
Share price (USD)	54.67
Number of outstanding shares (in million)	271

Solution

Market value of equity = $54.67 × 271 million

$\qquad\qquad\qquad\quad$ = $14,816 million

Market debt ratio = $5,475 million/($5,475 million + $14,816 million)

$\qquad\qquad\qquad$ = 26.98%

Debt ratio = $5,475 million /($5,475 million+$767 million)

$\qquad\quad$ = 87.7%

In this situation the traditional debt ratio and the market debt ratio both suggest conflicting possibilities. Debt ratio of 87.7% is quite alarming as it means that for roughly $9 of debt there is only $1 of equity and this is very risky for the debt-holders. Market debt ratio of 26.98% is quite safe on the other hand, as it suggests that the company is in a very comfortable solvency situation.

The extremely high debt ratio might be due to excessive adjustments to shareholders' equity resulting in very low equity at the period end and hence the very high debt ratio. Market debt ratio on the other hand takes into account the market valuation of the company and should be given more weight.

NET PROFIT MARGIN

Net profit margin (also called profit margin) is the most basic profitability ratio that measures the percentage of net income of an entity to its net sales. It represents the proportion of sales that is left over after all relevant expenses have been adjusted.

Net profit margin is used to compare profitability of competitors in the same industry. It can also be used to determine the profitability potential of different industries. While companies in some industries are able to generate high net profit margin, other industries offer very narrow margins. It depends on the extent of competition, elasticity of demand, production differentiation, etc. of the relevant product or market.

Return on equity and return on assets are other relevant ratios that measure the relationship of net income with shareholders' equity and total assets respectively.

Formula

$$\text{Net Profit Margin} = \frac{\text{Net Income}}{\text{Net Sales}}$$

Net Sales = Gross Sales − Sales Tax − Discounts − Sales Returns

Example

Following is an extract from Yahoo Finance (obtained on December 12, 2013) related to revenue and net income for the trailing twelve months (ttm) of The Goldman Sachs Group (NYSE: GS), JPMorgan Chase & Co. (NYSE:JPM), Morgan Stanley (NYSE: MS), and the financial services industry. Calculate their net profit margins and compare with relevant gross and operating margins.

All amounts are in USD in billion.

	GS	JPM	MS
Revenue	34.66	96.33	31.59
Net income	8.28	16.98	3.28
Gross margin	0.91	—	0.89
Operating margin	0.39	0.39	0.27

Solution

	GS	JPM	MS
Revenue	34.66	96.33	31.59
Net income	8.28	16.98	3.28
Net profit margin	**23.89%**	**17.63%**	**10.38%**

The table above shows that GS is the most profitable of the three companies. It managed to convert 23.89% of its sales into net income. JPM earned $17.63 net income per $100 of revenue. MS is the least profitable and generated 10.38% net profit margin.

OPERATING CYCLE

Operating cycle is the number of days a company takes in realizing its inventories in cash. It equals the time taken in selling inventories plus the time taken in recovering cash from trade receivables. It is called operating cycle because this process of producing/purchasing inventories, selling them, recovering cash from customers, using that cash to purchase/produce inventories and so on is repeated as long as the company is in operations. Operating cycle is a measure of the operating efficiency and working capital management of a company. A short operating cycle is good as it tells that the company's cash is tied up for a shorter period.

Another useful measure used to assess the operating efficiency of a company is the cash cycle (also called the cash conversion cycle).

Formula

Operating Cycle = Days' Sales of Inventory + Days Sales Outstanding

Days sales of inventory equals the average number of days in which a company sells its inventory. Day's sales outstanding on the other hand, is the period in which receivables are realized in cash.

An alternate expanded formula for operating income is as follows:

$$\text{Operating Cycle} = \frac{365}{\text{Purchases}} \times \text{Average Inventories} + \frac{365}{\text{Credit Sales}} \times \text{Average Accounts Receivable}$$

Example

Walmart Stores Inc. (NYSE: WMT) is all about inventories. Find its operating cycle assuming all sales are (a) cash sales and (b) credit sales. You can use cost of revenue as approximate figure for purchases (i.e. no need to adjust it for changes in inventories).

	USD in million
Revenue	469,162
Cost of revenue	352,488
Inventories as at 31 January 2013	43,803
Inventories as at 31 January 2012	40,714
Average inventories	42,259
Accounts receivable as at 31 January 2013	6,768
Accounts receivable as at 31 January 2012	5,937
Average accounts receivable	6,353

Solution

Part (a)

Days taken in converting inventories to accounts receivable = 365/352,488*42,259 = 43.75

Since there are no credit sales, times taken in recovering cash from accounts receivable is zero. Customers pay cash right away.

Operating cycle is 43.75 days and this represents the time taken in selling inventories.

Part (b)

There is no change in days taken in converting inventories to accounts receivable.

Days taken in converting receivables to cash = 365/469,162*6,353 = 4.92

Operating cycle = days taken in selling + days taken in recovering cash
$$= 43.75 + 4.92 = 48.68$$
It should be compared with operating cycle of Walmart Competitors, like Amazon, Costco, Target.

OPERATING MARGIN RATIO

Operating margin ratio or return on sales ratio is the ratio of operating income of a business to its revenue. It is profitability ratio showing operating income as a percentage of revenue.

Formula
Operating margin ratio is calculated by the following formula:

$$\text{Operating Margin} = \frac{\text{Operating Income}}{\text{Revenue}}$$

Operating income is same as earnings before interest and tax (EBIT). Both operating income and revenue figures can be obtained from the income statement of a business.

Analysis
Operating margin ratio of 9% means that a net profit of $0.09 is made on each dollar of sales. Thus a higher value of operating margin ratio is favourable which indicates that more proportion of revenue is converted to operating income. An increase in operating margin ratio overtime means that the profitability is improving. It is also important to compare the gross margin ratio of a business to the average gross profit margin of the industry. In general, a business which is more efficient is controlling its overall costs will have higher operating margin ratio.

Examples
Example 1: Determine the operating margin ratio of Company α given that its sales are $928,300 and its operating income is $113,200 for the month. What is the performance of the company compared to its industry which has average operating margin ratio of 10%?

Solution
Operating margin ratio = $113,200 / $928,300 ≈ 0.12 = 12%
The company is more profitable than an average firm in its industry.

Example 2: Calculate operating margin ratio from the following information:

Cost of Goods Sold	$34,390
Gross Profit	42,030
Other Operating Costs	37,200

Solution

Step 1: Revenue = $34,390 + $42,030

= $76,420

Step 2: Operating Income = $42,030 − $37,200

= $4,830

Step 3: Operating Margin Ratio = $4,830 / $76,420

≈ 0.063 or 6.3%

ACCOUNTS PAYABLE TURNOVER RATIO

Accounts payable turnover is the ratio of net credit purchases of a business to its average accounts payable during the period. It measures short term liquidity of business since it shows how many times during a period, an amount equal to average accounts payable is paid to suppliers by a business.

Formula

Accounts payable turnover is usually calculated as:

$$\text{Payables Turnover} = \frac{\text{Net Credit Purchases}}{\text{Average Accounts Payable}}$$

To calculate average accounts payable, divide the sum of accounts payable at the beginning and at the end of the period by 2. Net credit purchases figure in the denominator is not easily discoverable since such information is not usually available in financial statements. It is to be search for in the annual report of the company. Sometimes cost of goods sold is used in the denominator instead of credit purchases.

Analysis

Accounts payable turnover is a measure of short-term liquidity. A higher value indicates that the business was able to repay its suppliers quickly. Thus higher value of accounts payable turnover is favorable. This ratio can be of great importance to suppliers since they are interested in getting paid early for their supplies. Other things equal, a supplier should prefer to sell to a company with higher accounts payable turnover ratio.

Examples

Example 1: Company γ purchased goods having invoice value of $243,200 on credit during the year ended Dec 31, 2010. It returned goods costing $5,900 to suppliers. Accounts payable of the company on Jan 1, 2010 and Dec 31, 2011 were $23,000 and $34,900 respectively. Calculate its accounts payable ratio.

Solution

Net Credit Purchases = $243,200 − $5,900 = $237,300

Average Accounts Payable = ($23,000 + $34,900) / 2 = $28,950

Accounts Payable Turnover Ratio = $237,300 / $28,950 ≈ 8.2

PRICE PER EARNINGS (P/E) RATIO

Price per Earnings or P/E ratio is the ratio of a company's share price to its earnings per share. It tells whether the share price of a company is fairly valued, undervalued or overvalued.

Formula

$$\text{P/E Ratio} = \frac{\text{Current Share Price}}{\text{Earnings per Share}}$$

Current share price is obtained from secondary markets like NYSE, NASDAQ, etc. while EPS is calculated as (net income minus preferred dividends)/weighted average number of shares outstanding.

LEADING AND TRAILING PRICE PER EARNING RATIO

If the EPS is the figure for the current period the P/E ratio is called trailing P/E ratio. For better analysis the EPS should be the one expected to prevail in the next reporting period, say next year. P/E ratio calculated based on expected P/E ratio is called leading P/E and is a more meaningful estimate of the company's justified P/E ratio.

Analysis

For financial analysis justified P/E ratio is calculated using dividend discount method.

$$\text{P/E Ratio} = \frac{\text{Expected Payout Ratio}}{\text{Required Rate of Return} - \text{Dividend Growth Rate}}$$

If the justified P/E calculated using dividend discount analysis is higher than the current P/E ratio the share is undervalued and should be purchased. If the justified P/E is lower than P/E ratio the share is overvalued and should be sold.

Example

A share of T Ltd. has current market price of $20 and it's EPS for current period is reported as $2. It's EPS for next period is expected as $2.5, expected payout ratio is 40%, required rate of return is 12% and growth rate is 6%. Find the trailing P/E, leading P/E and justified P/E.

Solution

Trailing P/E = current share price/current year EPS

         = $20/$2

         = 10

Leading P/E = current share price/next year EPS

         = $20/$2.5

         = 8

Justified P/E = payout ratio/(required rate of return − growth rate)

         = 40%/(12% − 6%) = 40%/6% = 6.67

Reciprocal of P/E ratio is called earnings yield (which is EPS/price).

QUICK RATIO

Quick ratio or Acid Test ratio is the ratio of the sum of cash and cash equivalents, marketable securities and accounts receivable to the current liabilities of a business. It measures the ability of a company to pay its debts by using its cash and near cash current assets (i.e. accounts receivable and marketable securities).

Formula

Quick ratio is calculated using the following formula:

$$\text{Quick Ratio} = \frac{\text{Cash} + \text{Marketable Securities} + \text{Receivables}}{\text{Current Liabilities}}$$

Marketable securities are those securities which can be converted into cash quickly. Examples of marketable securities are treasury bills, saving bills, shares of stock-exchange, etc. Receivables refer to accounts receivable. Alternatively, quick ratio can also be calculated using the following formula:

$$\text{Quick Ratio} = \frac{\text{Current Assets} - \text{Inventory} - \text{Prepayments}}{\text{Current Liabilities}}$$

$$\text{Quick Ratio} = \frac{\text{Quick Assets}}{\text{Current Liabilities}}$$

Quick Assets = Current Assets - Inventories

Analysis

Quick ratio measures the liquidity of a business by matching its cash and near cash current assets with its total liabilities. It helps us to determine whether a business would be able to pay off all its debts by using its most liquid assets (i.e. cash, marketable securities and accounts receivable).

A quick ratio of 1.00 means that the most liquid assets of a business are equal to its total debts and the business will just manage to repay all its debts by using its cash, marketable securities and accounts receivable. A quick ratio of more than one indicates that the most liquid assets of a business exceed its total debts. On the opposite side, a quick ratio of less than one indicates that a business would not be able to repay all its debts by using its most liquid assets.

Thus we conclude that, generally, a higher quick ratio is preferable because it means greater liquidity. However a quick ratio which is quite high, say 4.00, is not favorable to a business as whole because this means that the business has idle current assets which could have been used to create additional projects thus increasing profits. In other words, very high value of quick ratio may indicate inefficiency.

Examples

Example 1: A company has following assets and liabilities at the year ended December 31, 2009:

Cash	$34,390
Marketable Securities	12,000
Accounts Receivable	56,200
Prepaid Insurance	9,000
Total Current Assets	111,590
Total Current Liabilities	73,780

Calculate quick ratio (acid test ratio).

Solution

Quick ratio = (34,390 + 12,000 + 56,200) / 73,780
　　　　　 = 102,590 / 73,780
　　　　　 = 1.39

OR

Quick ratio = (111,590 − 9,000) / 73,780
　　　　　 = 102,590 / 73,780
　　　　　 = 1.39

Example 2: Calculate quick ratio from the following information:

Cash	$21,720
Treasury Bills	18,500
Accounts Receivable	15,930
Prepaid Rent	6,500
Inventory	17,240
Total Current Assets	79,890
Total Current Liabilities	52,960

Solution

In this example, treasury bills are marketable securities thus we will calculate quick ratio as follows:

Quick ratio = (79,890 − 6,500 − 17,240) / 52,960
　　　　　 = 56,150 / 52,960
　　　　　 = 1.06

OR

Quick ratio = (21,720 + 18,500 + 15,930) / 52,960
　　　　　 = 56,150 / 52,960
　　　　　 = 1.06

ACCOUNTS RECEIVABLE TURNOVER RATIO

Accounts receivable turnover is the ratio of net credit sales of a business to its average accounts receivable during a given period, usually a year. It is an activity ratio which estimates the number of times a business collects its average accounts receivable balance during a period.

Formula

Accounts receivable turnover is calculated using the following formula:

$$\text{Receivables Turnover} = \frac{\text{Net Credit Sales}}{\text{Average Accounts Receivable}}$$

We can obtain the net credit sales figure from the income statement of a company. Average accounts receivable figure may be calculated simply by dividing the sum of beginning and ending accounts receivable by 2. The beginning and ending accounts receivable can be found on the balance sheets of the first and the last day of the accounting period.

Accounts receivable turnover is usually calculated on annual basis; however for the purpose of creating trends, it is more meaningful to calculate it on monthly or quarterly basis.

Analysis

Accounts receivable turnover measures the efficiency of a business in collecting its credit sales. Generally a high value of accounts receivable turnover is favourable and lower figure may indicate inefficiency in collecting outstanding sales. Increase in accounts receivable turnover overtime generally indicates improvement in the process of cash collection on credit sales.

However, a normal level of receivables turnover is different for different industries. Also, very high values of this ratio may not be favourable, if achieved by extremely strict credit terms since such policies may repel potential buyers.

Examples

Example 1: Net credit sales of Company A during the year ended June 30, 2010 were $644,790. Its accounts receivable at July 1, 2009 and June 30, 2010 were $43,300 and $51,730 respectively. Calculate the receivables turnover ratio.

Solution

Average Accounts Receivable = ($43,300 + $51,730) ÷ 2 = $47,515
Receivables Turnover Ratio = $644,790 ÷ $47,515 ≈ 13.57

Example 2: Total sales of Company B during the year ended December 31, 2010 were $984,000. Customers returned goods invoiced at $31,400 during the year. Average accounts receivable during the period were $23,880. Calculate accounts receivable turnover ratio.

Solution

Net Credit Sales = $984,000 − $31,400 = $952,600

Receivables Turnover = $952,600 ÷ $23,880 ≈ 39.89

RETENTION RATE (PLOWBACK RATIO)

Retention rate (also known as plowback ratio) is the ratio of earnings for the year retained to total earnings for the period. It is a measure of how much of the total earnings for a period a company is reinvesting as compared with paying out to shareholders.

Formula

$$\text{Retention Rate} = \frac{\text{Earnings Retained}}{\text{Total Earnings}}$$

Retention rate can also be calculated as 1 minus payout ratio.

Analysis

Companies normally retain a portion of earnings for future profitable capital expenditures. Retention rate tells the degree of such retention. Higher the retention rate higher will be the company's sustainable growth rate and higher share price.

Example

Zeta Ltd. earned an EPS of $2 in FY 2011 when it paid $1 per share as dividends. Find its retention rate.

Solution

Retention Rate = 1 − payout ratio

$\qquad\qquad$ = 1 − $1 / $2

$\qquad\qquad$ = 1 − 50%

$\qquad\qquad$ = 50%

RETURN ON ASSETS (ROA) RATIO

Return on assets is the ratio of annual net income to average total assets of a business during a financial year. It measures efficiency of the business in using its assets to generate net income. It is a profitability ratio.

Formula

The formula to calculate return on assets is:

$$\text{ROA} = \frac{\text{Annual Net Income}}{\text{Average Total Assets}}$$

Average Total Assets = (Beginning Total Assets + Ending Total Assets) / 2

$\quad$ Net income is the after tax income. It can be found on income statement. Average total assets are calculated by dividing the sum of total assets at the beginning and at the end of the financial year by 2. Total assets at the beginning and at the end of the year can be obtained from year ending balance sheets of two consecutive financial years.

Analysis

Return on assets indicates the number of cents earned on each dollar of assets. Thus higher values of return on assets show that business is more profitable. This ratio should be only used to compare companies in the same industry. The reason for this is that companies in some industries are most asset-insensitive i.e. they need expensive plant and equipment to generate income compared to others. Their ROA will naturally be lower than the ROA of companies which are low asset-insensitive. An increasing trend of ROA indicates that the profitability of the company is improving. Conversely, a decreasing trend means that profitability is deteriorating.

Examples

Example 1: Total assets of Company X on July 1, 2010 and June 30, 2011 were $2,132,000 and $2,434,000 respectively. During the year ended June 30, 2011 it earned net income of $213,000. Calculate its return on assets ratio.

Solution

Average Total Assets = ($2,132,000 + $2,434,000) / 2 = $2,283,000
Return on Assets = $213,000 / $2,283,000 ≈ 0.09 or 9%

Example 2: Total liabilities and total equity of Company Y on Dec 31, 2010 were $942,000 and $1,610,000 respectively. During the year ended Dec 31, 2010 the company earned net income of $315,000. What were the total assets of the company on Jan 1, 2010 given that its ROA for the year was 0.12

Solution

Step 1: Average Total Assets = Net Income / ROA = $315,000 / 0.12 = $2,625,000
Step 2: Ending Total Assets = $942,000 + $1,610,000 = $2,552,000
Step 3: Beginning Total Assets = (2 × $2,625,000) − $2,552,000 = $2,698,000

RETURN ON CAPITAL EMPLOYED (ROCE)

Return on capital employed (ROCE) is the ratio of net operating profit of a company to its capital employed. It measures the profitability of a company by expressing its operating profit as a percentage of its capital employed. Capital employed is the sum of stockholders' equity and long-term finance. Alternatively, capital employed can be calculated as the difference between total assets and current liabilities. The formula to calculate return on capital employed is:

$$ROCE = \frac{\text{Net Operating Profit}}{\text{Capital Employed}}$$

A more accurate value can be calculated by using average capital employed which is the sum of average long-term finance and average stockholders' equity.

Some analysts use earnings before interest and tax (EBIT) instead of net profit while calculating return on capital employed.

Since ROCE includes long-term finance in the calculation, therefore it is more comprehensive test of profitability as compared to return on equity (ROE).

Analysis

A higher value of return on capital employed is favorable indicating that the company generates more earnings per dollar of capital employed. A lower value of ROCE indicates lower profitability. A company having less assets but same profit as its competitors will have higher value of return on capital employed and thus higher profitability.

Examples

The average stockholders' equity and average capital employed of a company during the accounting year ended December 31, 20X2 were $348,000 and $120,000 respectively. The net profit during the period was $49,000. Calculate return on capital employed of the company.

Solution

Return on Capital Employed = 49,000 ÷ (348,000 + 120,000) = 10.5%

RETURN ON EQUITY (ROE) RATIO

Return on equity or return on capital is the ratio of net income of a business during a year to its stockholders' equity during that year. It is a measure of profitability of stockholders' investments. It shows net income as percentage of shareholder equity.

Formula

The formula to calculate return on equity is:

$$ROE = \frac{\text{Annual Net Income}}{\text{Average Stockholders' Equity}}$$

Average Stockholders' Equity = (Beginning Stockholders' Equity + Ending Stockholders' Equity) / 2

Net income is the after tax income whereas average shareholders' equity is calculated by dividing the sum of shareholders' equity at the beginning and at the end of the year by 2. The net income figure is obtained from income statement and the shareholders' equity is found on balance sheet. You will need year ending balance sheets of two consecutive financial years to find average shareholders' equity.

Analysis

Return on equity is an important measure of the profitability of a company. Higher values are generally favourable meaning that the company is efficient in generating income on new investment. Investors should compare the ROE of different companies and also check the trend in ROE over time. However, relying solely on ROE for investment decisions is not safe. It can be artificially influenced by the management, for example, when debt financing is used to reduce share capital there will be an increase in ROE even if income remains constant.

Examples

Example 1: Company A earned net income of $1,722,000 during the year ending march 31, 2011. The shareholders' equity on April 30, 2010 and March 31, 2011 was $14,587,000 and $16,332,000 respectively. Calculate its return on equity for the year ending March 31, 2011.

Solution

Average Shareholders' Equity = ($14,587,000 + $16,332,000) / 2 = $15,459,500
Return On Equity = $1,722,000 / $15,459,500 ≈ 0.11 or 11%

Example 2: Total assets and total liabilities of Company B on Jan 1, 2010 were $2,342,000 and $1,383,000. During the year ended December 31, 2011 it made a net profit of $242,000 and its shareholders' equity increased by $302,000. Calculate ROE of Company B.

Solution

Step 1: Beginning Shareholders' Equity = $2,342,000 − $1,383,000 = $959,000
Step 2: Ending Shareholders' Equity = $959,000 + $302,000 = $1,261,000
Step 3: Average Shareholders' Equity = ($959,000 + $1,261,000) / 2 = $1,110,000
Step 4: Return On Equity = $242,000 / $1,110,000 ≈ 0.22 or 22%

TIMES INTEREST EARNED RATIO

Times interest earned (also called interest coverage ratio) is the ratio of earnings before interest and tax (EBIT) of a business to its interest expense during a given period. It is a solvency ratio measuring the ability of a business to pay off its debts.

Formula

Times interest earned ratio is calculated as follows:

$$\text{Times Interest Earned} = \frac{\text{Earnings before Interest and Tax}}{\text{Interest Expense}}$$

Both figures in the above formula can be obtained from the income statement of a company. Earnings before interest and tax (EBIT) are same as operating income.

Analysis

Higher value of times interest earned ratio is favourable meaning greater ability of a business to repay its interest and debt. Lower values are unfavourable. A ratio of 1.00 means that income before interest and tax of the business is just enough to pay off its interest expense. That is why times interest earned ratio is of special importance to creditors. They can compare the debt repayment ability of similar companies using this ratio. Other things equal, a creditor should lend to a company with highest times interest earned ratio. It is also beneficial to create a trend of times interest earned ratio.

Examples
Example 1: Calculate the times interest earned ratio of a company having interest expense and earnings before interest and tax for the year ended Dec 31, 2010 of $239,000 and $3,493,000 respectively.

Solution
Times Interest Earned = $3,493,000 ÷ $239,000 ≈ 14.6

Example 2: The times interest earned ratio and earnings before interest and tax of a company were 9.34 and $1,324,400 during the year ended Jun 30, 2011. Calculate the interest expense of the company.

Solution
Interest Expense = $1,324,400 ÷ 9.34 ≈ $141,800

MULTIPILER

Multiplier is the ratio of ultimate change in GDP to initial change in spending and it is represented using the following formula:

$$\text{Multiplier} = \frac{\text{Change in Real GDP}}{\text{Initial Change in Spending}}$$

Reordering the above formula, we get,

Change in Real GDP = Multiplier × Change in Initial Spending

So if an increase of $50 billion in investment increases real GDP by a multiplier of 5, the real GDP will increase by $250 billion [= 50×5]. In this example, the multiplier effect is positive but it can also occur in other direction as well i.e. decrease in initial spending reducing real GDP by multiple times of initial decrease in spending.

MULTIPLIER EFFECT

Multiplier effect is a macro-economic phenomenon in which an initial change in spending results in a greater ultimate change in real GDP. The initial change is usually a change in investment but other components of GDP such as government spending, net exports and a change in consumption which is not caused by change in income can also have multiplier effect on the GDP.

Multiplier effect occurs under the assumption that the economy has room to expand so that increase in spending does not result solely in inflation.

Explanation

Since the money spent in an economy is received by others as income and assuming that an average person is likely to change their spending in direct proportion to their income, therefore an initial increase or decrease in spending will start a chain of increased or decreased spending by a number of people. The ultimate change in GDP will be the total of the incremental changes in spending of multiple people caused by the initial change in spending.

Consider the example given above where the initial change in investment is $50 billion. This initial investment increases GDP by $50 billion is first stage. The initial investment is received in the form of income by a number people. Provided that they consume 80% of their income and save the rest, $40 billion [=$50×0.8] of the initial investment will be spent in second stage. The amount spent in second stage is also received by other people as income. In third stage, $32 billion [=$40×0.8] will be spent. In forth stage, $25.6 billion [=$32×0.8] will be spent. If we continue this process long enough and add all the amounts together or, we can simply use the following formula to calculate the total of this convergent geometric series:

$$\text{Change in Real GDP} = \frac{\text{Initial Change in Spending}}{1 - \text{MPC}}$$

$$\text{Change in Real GDP} = \frac{\$50 \text{ billion}}{1 - 0.8} = \$250 \text{ billion}$$

As you may have noted, the multiplier is related to percentage of total income spent by people who directly or indirectly derive income from initial spending. This percentage is known as marginal propensity to consume.

EQUITY MULTIPLIER

Equity multiplier is a financial leverage ratio which is calculated by dividing total assets by the shareholders equity. It tells about assets in dollar per dollar of equity. The higher the ratio the lower the financial leverage and the lower the ratio the higher the financial leverage

Formula

$$\text{Equity Multiplier} = \frac{\text{Total Assets}}{\text{Total Equity}}$$

Equity multiplier is an important input in the DuPont return on equity analysis. DuPont return on equity analysis breaks up ROE into net profit margin, asset turnover and financial leverage (represented by equity multiplier as shown below:

ROE Under DuPont Analysis = $\dfrac{\text{Net Income}}{\text{Sales}} \times \dfrac{\text{Sales}}{\text{Total Assets}} \times \dfrac{\text{Total Assets}}{\text{Total Equity}} = \dfrac{\text{Net Income}}{\text{Total Equity}}$

Higher equity multiplier leads to a higher return on equity.

Examples

Example 1: Company EP has total assets of $100 billion, beginning equity of $40 billion, net income for the year of $10 billion and dividends paid during the year of $4 billion.

We calculate the equity multiplier as total assets divided by total equity.

Total assets are $100 billion

Total equity = beginning equity + net income – dividends = $40 b plus $10 b minus $4 b = $46 billion

Equity multiplier is hence $100 billion divided by $46 billion and it equals 2.2

Example 2: Company DP has debt to equity ratio of 2. Find the equity multiplier

Debt/Equity = 2

Since debt = assets minus equity

(Assets – Equity)/Equity = 2

Assets – Equity = 2 Equity

Assets = 3 Equity

Assets/Equity = 3

Hence, equity multiplier is 3.

For further analysis of equity multiplier as part of DuPont analysis refer to: DuPont Analysis.

WORKING CAPITAL

Working capital is a measure of liquidity of a business. It equals current assets minus current liabilities.

Formula

Working Capital = Current Assets – Current Liabilities

Current assets are assets that are expected to be realized in a year or within one operating cycle.

Current liabilities are obligations that are required to be paid within a year or within one operating cycle.

Analysis

If current assets of a business at the point in time are more than its current liabilities the working capital is positive, and this tells that the company is not expected to suffer from liquidity crunch in near future. However, if current assets are less than current liabilities the working capital is negative, and this communicates that the business may not be able to pay off its current liabilities when due.

Examples
1. Company A has current assets of USD 5 million and current liabilities of USD 3 million. Its working capital is USD 2 million (USD 5 million minus USD 3 million).
2. Company B has current ratio of 1.5 and its current liabilities are USD 80 million. Since current ratio is equal to current assets minus current liabilities we can calculate current assets by multiplying current ratio with current liabilities (USD 80 million*1.5=USD 120 million). Current liabilities are USD 80 million hence working capital is USD 120 million minus USD 80 million which equals USD 40 million.

WORKING CAPITAL TURNOVER

Working capital turnover ratio is an activity ratio that measures dollars of revenue generated per dollar of investment in working capital. Working capital is defined as the amount by which current assets exceed current liabilities.

A higher working capital turnover ratio is better. It means that the company is utilizing its working capital more efficiently i.e. generating more revenue using less investment.

Formula

$$\text{Working Capital Turnover Ratio} = \frac{\text{Revenue}}{\text{Average Working Capital}}$$

Working Capital = Current Assets − Current Liabilities

$$\text{Average Working Capital} = \frac{\text{Opening Working Capital} + \text{Closing Working Capital}}{2}$$

Example
Calculate and analyze the working capital turnover ratios of General Electric (NYSE: GE), United Technologies Corporation (NYSE: UTX) and Amazon Inc. (NYSE: AMZN) for financial year 2012. Relevant extracts from their financial statements are given below. All amounts are in USD in million.

	GE	UTX	AMZN
Revenue	147,359	57,708	70133
Current Assets	428,729	29,610	21296
Current Liabilities	221,403	23,786	19002

Solution

The following schedule contains the required calculations:

	GE	UTX	AMZN
Revenue (A)	147,359	57,708	70,133
Current Assets (B)	428,729	29,610	21,296
Current Liabilities (C)	221,403	23,786	19,002
Working capital (D)[= B − C]	207,326	5,824	2,294
Working capital turnover (A ÷ D)	0.71	9.91	30.57

Since GE and UTX are competitors, working capital turnover ratio can be used to compare their asset utilization. UTX is clearly using its investment in working capital more efficiently as indicated by its higher working capital turnover ratio when compared to GE's ratio. AMZN on the other hand is not a competitor of GE or UTX so comparison between GE/UTX and AMZN based on working capital turnover ratio is not appropriate.

Further, AMZN's industry and its market position is such that it can maintain very low working capital. In such a situation working capital turnover ratio is not very useful. Fixed asset turnover and total asset turnover ratio should be used in such scenarios.

CHAPTER THREE
SPECIALIZED / INDUSTRY-SPECIFIC RATIOS

OVER VIEW

Financial ratios are relationship and proportions between different items of data (both financial and non-financial) that can provide any insight into any aspect of a company's business. Some financial ratios such as current ratio, net profit margin, etc. are relevant to all companies and are hence widely used. Others are used either in a specific industry or for some very specific purpose of advanced nature such as valuation.

INDUSTRY SPECIFIC RATIOS

Industry-specific ratios are ratios that are useful only in a specific industry and hence calculated for analyzing entities in that industry only. These ratios are meaningless for entities in other industries. These include:
- Occupancy ratio for hoteling industry
- Capital adequacy ratio for banks
- Monetary reserve requirement for banks
- Sales per square foot for companies in retail business
- Revenue per employee for service companies

VALUATION RATIOS

Valuation ratios express relationships between share price of a company and some of the entity's other key statistics. For example price to book value per share, price to cash flow per share, etc. Such ratios are used to value a company's share relative to the value of another similar company.

CAPITAL ADEQUACY RATIO

Capital adequacy ratio (CAR) is a specialized ratio used by banks to determine the adequacy of their capital keeping in view their risk exposures. Banking regulators require a minimum capital adequacy ratio so as to provide the banks with a cushion to absorb losses before they become insolvent. This improves stability in financial markets and protects deposit-holders. Basel Committee on Banking Supervision of the Bank of International Settlements develops rules related to capital adequacy which member countries are expected to follow.
The committee's latest pronouncement on capital adequacy is Basel III, issued December 2010, revised June 2011. Complete text is available here.
The pronouncement requires banks to maintain the following minimum ratios as of 1 January 2013:

Common Equity Tier 1 ÷ Risk-weighted Exposures	3.5%
Tier 1 Capital ÷ Risk-weighted Exposures	4.5%
Total Capital ÷ Risk-weighted Exposures	8%

Since such pronouncements are frequently updated, please consult the Bank of International Settlements website for latest guidance.

Formula

$$\text{Capital Adequacy Ratio} = \frac{\text{Tier 1 Capital} + \text{Tier 2 Capital}}{\text{Risk-weighted Exposures}}$$

Tier 1 Capital = Common Equity Tier 1 + Additional Tier 1
Total Capital = Tier 1 Capital + Tier 2 Capital

Risk-weighted exposures include weighted sum of the banks credit exposures (including those appearing on the bank's balance sheet and those not appearing). The weights are determined in accordance with the Basel Committee guidance for assets of each credit rating slab.

Example

Calculate capital adequacy ratio i.e. total capital to risk weighted exposures ratio for Small Bank Inc. using the following information:

	Exposure	Risk Weight
Government Treasury held as asset	1,500,000	0%
Loans to Corporates	15,000,000	10%
Loans to Small Businesses	8,000,000	20%
Guarantees and other non-balance sheet exposures	6,000,000	10%

The bank's Tier 1 Capital and Tier 2 Capital are $200,000 and $300,000 respectively.

Solution

Banks's total capital = 200,000 + 300,000 = $500,000
Risk-weighted exposures = $1.5×0% + $15×10% + $8×20% + $6×10% = $3.7 million

$$\text{Capital Adequacy Ratio} = \frac{\$0.5 \text{ million}}{\$3.7 \text{ million}} = 14\%$$

If the national regulator requires a capital adequacy ratio of 10%, the bank is safe. However, if the required ratio is 15%, the bank might have to face regulatory actions.
Please note that guarantees and other non-balance sheet exposures are included in the calculation of risk-weighted exposures.

EBITDA COVERAGE RATIO

EBITDA coverage ratio is a solvency ratio that measures a company's ability to pay off its liabilities related to debts and leases. It compares the company's earnings before interest, tax, depreciation, amortization (EBITDA) plus lease payments to the sum of debt payments and lease payments.

EBITDA coverage ratio is broader than the times interest earned ratio, which measures a company's ability to pay interest charges on debt. EBITDA approximates a company's cash flows more closely than its earnings do (because it excludes non-cash expenses of depreciation and amortization). Since debts are to be repaid using the cash flows generated, EBITDA coverage is a useful measure of a company's ability to pay off its debt repayment obligations.

Formula

$$\text{EBITDA Coverage Ratio} = \frac{\text{EBITDA} + \text{Lease Payments}}{\text{Interest Payments} + \text{Principal Repayments} + \text{Lease Payments}}$$

Where EBITDA is Earnings Before Interest, Tax, Depreciation and Amortization. It can be calculated from net income as follows:
EBITDA = Net Income + Tax + Interest + Depreciation + Amortization

Example
Calculate EBITDA coverage ratio and times interest earned ratio for Company ABC using the following information:

Net income	2,000,000
Income tax expense	857,143
Interest expense	1,000,000
Lease payments	800,000
Principal repayment on debt	2,000,000
Depreciation	1,200,000
Amortization	900,000

The relevant industry average for EBITDA coverage and TIE is 2 and 3 respectively.

Solution
EBITDA = 2,000,000 + 857,143 + 1,000,000 + 1,200,000 + 900,000 = 5,957,143

$$\text{EBITDA Coverage Ratio} = \frac{5,957,143 + 800,000}{1,000,000 + 2,000,000 + 800,000} = 1.78$$

EBIT = 2,000,000 + 857,143 + 1,000,000 = 3,857,143

$$\text{Times Interest Earned} = \frac{3,857,143}{1,000,000} = 3.86$$

EBITDA coverage ratio of 1.78 means that the company can safely pay off its periodic debt repayment obligations. However, it is below the industry average.
Times interest earned ratio of 3.86 tells that the company has the capacity to pay almost 4 times the current interest expense, and it is better than the industry average.

PRICE TO BOOK RATIO

Price to book ratio (also called market to book ratio) is a relative valuation statistic which measures the proportion of the current market price of a share of a company's common stock to the book value per share of the company. Price to book value tells whether investors in general value the company above, at or below the face value of the company's assets as they appear in its financial reports.

Market value of a share is determined by the average opinion of the investors about the company. Book value on the other hand, is determined using accounting principles. There are a number of factors that are not captured by accounting information, for example, value of a company's brands, reputation, growth potential, etc. Such factors create divergence between the two figures and make price to book ratio a useful tool for finding investor feeling about a company's future outlook.

Investors who specialize in buying companies whose current market prices are suppressed place significant emphasis on price to book ratio. They buy companies with low price to book ratio but good return on equity and sell them when the market adjusts its opinion about the company's true worth. Price to book ratio can also be used to find out how much a company is worth by comparing its book value to the average price to book value of the industry or competitors.

Formula

$$\text{Price to Book Ratio} = \frac{\text{Current Share Price}}{\text{Book Value per Share}}$$

Book value per share can be calculated using the following formula:

$$\text{Book Value per Share} = \frac{\text{Total Shareholders' Equity}}{\text{Total Number of Shares Outstanding}}$$

P/B ratio can also be calculated using the following formula:

$$\text{Price to Book Ratio} = \frac{\text{Current Market Capitalization}}{\text{Total Shareholders' Equity}}$$

Example

Calculate price to book value for Kellogg Company (NYSE: K) and General Mills Inc. (NYSE: GIS) using the following information.
All figures other than per share values are in million US$.

	K	GIS
Relevant current market price	54	48
Total shareholders' equity	2,419	6,672
Number of shares outstanding	362	625

Solution

	K	GIS
Relevant current market price (P)	54	48
Total shareholders' equity (X)	2,419	6,672
Number of shares outstanding (Y)	362	625
Book value per share (B = X/Y)	6.68	10.68
Price to book ratio (P/B)	8.05	4.51

It tells that investors value $1 of net assets (assets minus liabilities) appearing on Kellogg's balance sheet almost as early as $2 of net assets of General Mills Inc. This must be supported by high return offered by Kellogg evidenced by for example high return on equity. If it is not the case, Kellogg's stock might be overvalued.

CASH FLOW PER SHARE

Cash flow per share is a financial ratio that measures the operating cash flows attributable to each share of common stock. It is a variation of the earnings per share which substitutes net income with net cash flows from operations. While net income is subject to management judgment and discretion in choice of accounting policies and preparation of accounting estimates, the net cash flows from operating activities is more concrete figure, and potentially more reliable.

Formula

$$\text{Cash flow per share} = \frac{\text{Cash Flows from Operating Activities} - \text{Preferred Dividends}}{\text{Weighted Average Number of Shares}}$$

Weighted average number of shares is a figure calculated by weighting each share by the proportion of the year for which it remained outstanding.

If a company prepares its financial statements in accordance with IFRS and classifies the dividend paid to common shareholders as cash out flow from operating activities, it must add back the common dividends to the net cash flows from operating activities because they are part of cash flows attributable to common shareholders.

Example

Following is an extract from financial statements of Holiday Travel and Tours for financial years 2013 and 2014 prepared in accordance with US GAAP. All amounts are in million USDs.

	2014	2013
Net income	210	190
Preferred dividends	20	44
Common dividends	50	60
Common shares at the start of the financial year	10	8

Common shares issued at the end of 2nd quarter   0   2
Cash flows from operating activities   150 110
  Cash flows from operating activities   150 110

Calculate cash flows per share for 2013 and 2014 and contrast it with earnings per share for the relevant years.

Solution
We need to calculate weighted average number of common shares for both years:

Weighted average common shares (2013) = $8 \times \dfrac{12}{12} + 2 \times \dfrac{6}{12} = 9$ million

Weighted average common shares (2014) = 10
2 million shares issued at the end of 2nd quarter of 2013 carries a weight of 50% representing the six (out of twelve) months for which they remained outstanding. There is no new issues in 2014, so the weighted average number of common shares for 2014 is equal to the opening common shares that remained outstanding for the whole year.

The following table summarizes the calculation of relevant ratios

	2014	2013
Net income	210	190
Less: preferred dividends	-20	-44
Income attributable to common shareholders	190	146
Weighted average number of common shares	10	9
Earnings per share (USD per share)	19.00	16.22
Net cash flows from operating activities	150	110
Less: preferred dividends	-20	-44
Net cash flows attributable to common shareholders	130	66
Weighted average number of common shares	10	9
Cash flow per share (USD per share)	13.00	7.33

EPS has increased over the year and this fact is supported by the increase in cash flow per share over the same period. It suggests that the increase is EPS is not just due to any accounting trick rather is supported by actual cash flows. As an investor, we will feel more confident in our analysis.

REVENUE PER EMPLOYEE

Revenue per employee (also called sales per employee) is a financial ratio that measures the revenue generated by each employee of the company on average. It equals the company's total revenue divided by the average number of employees for the period.
Revenue per employee is relevant for labour-intensive industries an i.e. industry in which human capital is more important than the physical capital for revenue generation.

A similar ratio is net income per employee, which measures net income earned by each employee on average.

Formula

$$\text{Revenue per Employee} = \frac{\text{Net Revenue}}{\text{Average Number of Employees}}$$

Example

Auditing, tax and consultancy are labor-intensive industries. The big four accounting firms are few of the world's largest professional services firms and their revenue depends exclusively on their human capital. Calculate the revenue per share for each using the data given below for financial year 2013.
Revenue in million US Dollars.

	Revenue	Employees
Deloitte	32,400	200,000
PwC	32,100	184,000
EY	25,800	175,000
KPMG	23,400	155,000

Solution

	Revenue	Employees	Revenue per Employee
Deloitte	32,400	200,000	162,000
PwC	32,100	184,000	174,457
EY	25,800	175,000	147,429
KPMG	23,400	155,000	150,968

SHAREHOLDERS' EQUITY

Shareholders' equity represents the interest of a company's shareholders in the net assets of the company. According to the accounting equation:

Shareholders' Equity = Assets − Liabilities

On a balance sheet, there is separate section for shareholders' equity which includes its components such as common stock, preferred stock, additional paid-up capital, accumulated other comprehensive income, treasury stock and retained earnings.
Common stock represents the legal capital of the company.
Preferred stock is a sort of share capital which has a preferred right to dividends.
Additional paid-up capital represents the cash contributed by the shareholders of the company in excess of the legal capital of the company i.e. the common stock.
Accumulated other comprehensive income represents the credits or debits in shareholders' equity which are other than those related to transactions with shareholders, for example credit

for revaluation surplus, credits and debits related to translation reserve, changes in fair value of available for sale investments, etc.

Treasury stock is contra-equity account which means that it appears as a deduction from other shareholders' equity accounts and it represents the cost of the company's investment in its own share stock.

Retained earnings represent the total earnings of the company retained by the company for reinvestment. It equals the retained earnings of last period plus net income for the period minus dividends paid during the period.

COMMON STOCK

Common stock is a component of shareholder equity on a company's balance sheet which represents the interest of the company's owners.

Unlike a sole proprietorship or a partnership (in which the capital is contributed by one or a limited number of people), companies are normally owned by hundreds and thousands of people. The share capital of companies is divided into large numbers of shares called common shares. A common share is evidence of ownership in a company and represents a right to its net assets. It makes transfer of ownership easy and is the prime reason for popularity of companies as a form of business.

PAR VALUE OF COMMON STOCK

A company normally assigns a value called par value to a share of its common stock and mentions it in the legal document. The figure might be $1 or $10 or $100 or just trivial. For example, the par value of a share of Microsoft is $0.00000625. However, it is not mandatory for a company to assign a par value. For example, Apples Inc. has no par value assigned to its shares.

STATED VALUE OF A COMMON STOCK

Stated value is a value attached to a share of common stock with no par value. Stated value per share is used to determine the legal capital of the company for accounting purposes.

AUTHORIZED CAPITAL

A company has to obtain authorization from the relevant securities regular regarding issue of share capital. Authorized capital is the number of shares which the company is authorized to issue.

ISSUED CAPITAL

Issued capital is the number of shares which the company has issued. It is lower or equal to the authorized capital.

OUTSTANDING CAPITAL

Outstanding capital is the issued capital of the company minus its treasury stock.

COMPREHENSIVE EXAMPLE

The common stock portion of the equity section of Apple Inc. balance sheet as at 24 September 2011 is given below:

Common stock (no par value):

Shares authorized	1,800,000
Shares issued and outstanding	929,277
Value in million Dollars	13,331

It provides the following information:
- The company has no par value stock.
- There is no stated value disclosed.
- Authorized share capital is 1.8 million shares.
- The company has issued roughly half of its authorized share capital as at 24 September 2011.
- The company has no treasury stock that is why shares issued and shares outstanding are equal.

Issuance of Shares of Stock

When companies need more capital, they issue new shares to investors. Usually, the shares are issued in exchange of cash or cash equivalents but they may be issued in exchange of other assets such as property, plant and equipment. The investor receives share certificates as evidence of contribution towards the capital of the company.

The journal entries to record the issuance of stocks depends on whether the shares have been issued at par value or not.

Issuance of Par Value Stock

Par value shares are those which have a face value assigned to them. Such shares may be issued at par, above par or below par.

When par value shares are issued exactly at par, cash is debited and common stock or preferred stock account is credited.

In case of issuance above par, cash account is debited for the total cash received by the company, common stock or preferred stock is credited for the par value multiplied by number shares issued and additional paid-in capital account is credited for the excess of cash received over the par value multiplied by number of shares issued.

When par value shares are issued below par, cash is debited for the actual amount received, common stock or preferred stock is credited for the total par value and discount on capital is debited for the excess of total par value over cash received. The discount on capital is part of shareholders' equity and it appears as a deduction from other equity accounts on balance sheet.

ISSUANCE OF NO PAR STOCK

Issuance of shares having no par value is recorded by debiting cash and crediting common stock or preferred stock. However if board of directors of the company assigns a value to shares orally, such value is called stated value and the journal entries will be similar to par value stock

Example

A company received $34,000 for issuing 10,000 shares of common stock of $3 par value. Pass the journal entry to record the issuance of shares.
Journal Entry

Cash	34,000	
Common Stock		30,000
Additional Paid-In Capital		4,000

ISSUANCE OF SHARES FOR NON-CASH ITEMS

Corporations usually issue shares in exchange of cash or cash equivalents since cash can be used to purchase other assets or services. However shares may be issued in exchange of non-cash assets or services if the company actually needs them. For example shares may be issued to the supplier of machinery as purchase price and to attorneys as legal fee.
Generally such transactions of share issuance are recorded at the fair market value of the shares or the non-cash assets/services which ever can be determined more reliably. The determination of fair market value is the right of the board of directors of the company and they may obtain services of professional appraisers for to determine the fair market value.

Example

A company issued 1,000 shares of common stock of $10 par value to its attorney as a consideration for legal services received by the company. The total fair market value of the shares, which was $9,800 at the time of issuance of shares, is to be used as the basis for valuation of the legal services.
Pass a journal entry to record the issuance of shares for non-cash consideration.

ISSUANCE OF SHARES FOR NON-CASH ITEMS

Corporations usually issue shares in exchange of cash or cash equivalents since cash can be used to purchase other assets or services. However shares may be issued in exchange of non-cash assets or services if the company actually needs them. For example shares may be issued to the supplier of machinery as purchase price and to attorneys as legal fee.
Generally such transactions of share issuance are recorded at the fair market value of the shares or the non-cash assets/services which ever can be determined more reliably. The determination of fair market value is the right of the board of directors of the company and they may obtain services of professional appraisers for to determine the fair market value.

Example

A company issued 1,000 shares of common stock of $10 par value to its attorney as a consideration for legal services received by the company. The total fair market value of the shares, which was $9,800 at the time of issuance of shares, is to be used as the basis for valuation of the legal services.

Pass a journal entry to record the issuance of shares for non-cash consideration.

Journal Entry

Legal Expense	9,800	
Common Stock		10,000
Additional Paid-In Capital		200

LUMP-SUM STOCK ISSUANCE

A corporation may issue different types of stocks in a single transaction in exchange of a lump-sum of cash or other assets or services. For example, common stock and preferred stock may be issued in exchange of a single sum of cash or machinery. To record such transactions it is necessary to determine the portion of lump-sum cash or the value of property obtained to be allocated to each class of stock.

Usually the lump-sum amount is apportioned to each class of stock issued on the basis of the market values of each class of stock. This method is called the apportionment method. It uses the following formula to calculate the amount of lump-sum to be allocated to each class of stock:

$$\text{Apportionment} = \frac{A}{B} \times C$$

Where,

A is the market value of a particular class of stock issued for lump-sum;

B is the total market value of all the stocks issued for lump-sum; and

C is the lump-sum cash received or, in case of some other asset or service, its fair market value.

When two classes of stocks have been issued for a lump-sum and the market value of one class is known and that of the other is unknown, then the incremental method should be employed. According to incremental method, the portion of lump-sum equal to the stock's market value would be allocated to that class of stock and rest will be allocated to the other class.

Once the amount to be apportioned to each class of stock is calculated, the issuance of stocks is recorded via separate journal entries for each class of stock in such a way as if there had been separate transactions for each class of stock. This is illustrated the following example:

Example

A company issued 3,000 shares of $6 par value common stock and 1,000 shares of $10 par value preferred stock for a lump-sum of $56,000. On the day of issuance of the stocks for lump-sum, the market values per share of common stock and preferred stock were $10 and $20 respectively.

Apportion the lump-sum to common stock and preferred stock.

Solution

	Market Value	
Common Stock	$30,000	3/7 × $56,000 = $24,000
Preferred Stock	$40,000	4/7 × $56,000 = $32,000
	$70,000	

Journal Entries:

Cash	24,000	
Common Stock		18,000
Additional Paid-In Capital		6,000
Cash	32,000	
Preferred Stock		20,000
Additional Paid-In Capital		12,000

COST METHOD

Cost method is one of the two methods of accounting for treasury stock, the stock which has been bought back by the issuing company itself. The other method is called the par value method.

Under the cost method, the purchase of treasury stock is recorded by debiting treasury stock account by the actual cost of purchase. The cost method ignores the par value of the shares and the amount received from investors when the shares were originally issued.

When treasury shares are later reissued, the treasury stock account is credited for the cost at which they were purchased, cash account is debited for the amount actually received and if the amount received on reissuance of treasury stock is:

- More than the cost of treasury stock, the difference between the amount received and the cost of the treasury stock is credited to additional paid-in capital.
- Less than the cost of treasury stock, the excess of cost of treasury stock over the amount received is debited to discount on capital account.

The following example illustrates the cost method of accounting for treasury stock:

Example

A company issued 10,000 shares of common stock of $5 par value and received $53,000 cash. The company then purchased back 900 shares out of those at $6 per share. The company then resold 500 shares from treasury stock at $6.50 per share.

Pass journal entries to record the above transactions.

Solution

Issuance of Common Stock:

Cash	53,000	
Common Stock		50,000
Additional Paid-In Capital		3,000

Purchase of Treasury Stock (Cost Method):

Treasury Stock	5,400	
Cash		5,400

Resale of Treasury Stock (Cost Method):

Cash	3,250	
Treasury Stock		3,000
Additional Paid-In Capital		250

PAR VALUE METHOD

Par value method of accounting for treasury stock is one of the two techniques of accounting to record the purchase and resale of treasury stock. Treasury stock refers to shares which have been bought by the issuing company itself.

Under par value method, purchase of treasury stock is recorded by debiting treasury stock by the total par value of the shares. Cash account is credited for the actual amount paid to purchase the treasury stock. Any additional paid-in capital or discount on capital relating to treasury shares is cancelled by a debit or credit respectively. At this point, if the sum of credit side of the journal entry is less than the sum of debit side, additional paid-in capital account will be credited for the difference. Alternatively if the sum of credit side exceeds the sum of debit side of the journal entry, the difference will be debited to additional paid-in capital account up to the available balance and the rest, if any, will be debited to retained earnings account.

The resale of treasury stock is recorded by debiting cash account for the actual amount received, crediting treasury stock for the par value of the treasury shares and if the cash received on resale is:

- More than the total par value of treasury shares, the excess is credited to additional paid-in capital account.
- Less than the total par value of treasury shares, the difference is debited to additional paid-in capital from treasury stock provided it has sufficient credit balance otherwise retained earnings account is debited.

The following example shows the journal entries to record the purchase and resale of treasury stock under par value method.

Example

A corporation issued 12,000 shares of common stock of $4 par value and received $57,000 from investors. It then bought back 1,000 of the shares and paid a sum of $4,500 for the purchase. Later it resold 500 of the treasury shares at a price of $5 per share.
Journalize the above transactions according the par value method of accounting for treasury stock.

Solution
Issuance of Common Stock:

Cash	57,000	
Common Stock		48,000
Additional Paid-In Capital		9,000

Purchase of Treasury Stock (Par Value Method):

Treasury Stock	4,000	
Additional Paid-in Capital[1]	750	
Cash		4,500
Add. Paid-in Capital from TS[2]		250

1: $9,000 \times (1,000 \div 12,000)$
2: $4,000 + 750 - 4,500$

Resale of Treasury Stock (Par Value Method):

Cash	2,500	
Treasury Stock		2,000
Additional Paid-In Capital		500

STOCK DIVIDENDS

Stock dividends (also called bonus shares) represent the distribution of retained earnings to investors in the form of additional shares in the company instead of cash.
When companies have high retained earning but they do not have necessary excess cash, they resort to issuing stock dividends. Another motivation to issue stock dividends is to bring down the stock price in the market. Introduction of additional shares in the market without any increase in the company's value reduces the company's share price. Companies want to reduce their share price in order to bring down their price to earnings ratio and encourage investors to hold the company's shares.
When the board of directors of a company declares a 10% stock dividend it means that additional shares equivalent to 10% of the current shares are to be issued to the shareholders. The accounting for stock dividend depends on whether it is considered to be a large stock dividend of a small one.

SMALL STOCK DIVIDEND

If the stock dividend is less than 20-25%, it is a small stock dividend and is accounted for by the journal entries explained below:

i. At the time of declaration, retained earnings is debited by the amount equal to the product of the share's market price, the stock dividend percentage and the current number of shares outstanding; and stock dividends distributable is credited by the same amount.

ii. At the time of issuance of stock the stock dividends distributable is debited by the full amount, common stock is credited by amount equal to the product of par value per share, stock dividend percentage and the number of current shares outstanding. Any excess of stock dividends distributable over the amount credited to common stock is credit to additional paid-in capital.

LARGE STOCK DIVIDEND

If the stock dividend declared is more than 20%-25%, it is a large stock dividend and is more like a stock split. In this case, declaration is recorded by debiting retained earnings by the product of par value per share, percentage of stock dividend and number of outstanding shares; and crediting stock dividends distributable. At the time of issuance, the stock dividends distributable are debited and common stock is credited.

Example

A company has 200,000 outstanding shares of common stock of $10 par value. It declares 10% stock dividend. The market price per share of common stock was $15 on the date of declaration.

Record the declaration and payment of the stock dividend using journal entries.

Solution

Journal entry on the date of declaration:

Retained Earnings	300,000	
Stock Dividends Distributable		300,000

Journal entry on the date of distribution:

Stock Dividends Distributable	300,000	
Common Stock		200,000
Addition Paid-In Capital		100,000

STOCK SPLITS

Stock split is the issuance of additional shares by a company to its shareholders without receiving any related contribution from them. Such an issue increases the number of shares issued and outstanding without increasing the total balance of common stock and market capitalization of the company. The effect of stock split is to split the par value and market price per share. In fact, the sole purpose of the stock split is to reduce the market price per share so as to make it more attractive for investors.

Stock splits are designed by companies in regard to their intended effect on the market price. If a company wants to reduce its market price to half it will issue 2-for-1 stock split which means the company shall issue addition 1 share per 1 share currently issued and outstanding thereby doubling the total number of shares. There might be a 3-for-2 stock split, for example, which means that 3 shares are to be issued for each 2 shares of currently issues shares.

Stock split has no effect on balance of any equity account. It just increases the number of shares and reduces par value.

Example

Z Ltd. has 2 million of $10 par value common stock issued and outstanding which is currently trading at $300 per share. The management believes that the share price is too high and it intends to reduce it to its 1/3.

The company would need to issue a 3-for-1 stock split which means that for each of currently issued common shares the company shall issue 3 shares. It will increase the total number of shares issued and outstanding to 6 million (2 million × 3) resulting in a par value of $3.33 ($10 ÷ 3) and a market price of $100 ($300 ÷ 33).

It will not affect balance in any of the accounts.

RETAINED EARNINGS

A company either pays out its earnings for a period or it retains it to fuel internal growth. Retained earnings are the equity account which holds those accumulated retained earnings. Retained earnings are affected by net income for the period, dividends paid out during the period, etc. Other adjustments to retained earnings include adjustment related to changes in accounting policies and estimates, etc.

Retained earnings statement report changes in retained earnings in a period.

Example

IG Plc. has a balance in retained earnings as at 1 January 2011 of $102 million. It earned a net income of $40 million for the year and declared dividends of $45 million in the year. The statement of retained earnings would look like as follows:

Retained earnings as at 1 January 2011	$102 million
Plus: net income for the period	$40 million
Less: dividends declared	-$45 million
Retained earnings as at 31 December 2011	$97 million

Non-Current Liabilities

Long-term liabilities (also known as non-current liabilities) are obligations which a business is expected to pay in the next year or in the next operating cycle. These include bonds payable, notes payable, liabilities related to pension benefits, leases, etc.

Example

Company A is has the following obligations as at 31 December 2011:

1. Lease payable of $10 million (of which $1 is expected to be paid in 6 months and the rest afterwards).

2. Net pension liability of $20 million (of which $2 payable in the current operating cycle).

3. Bonds payable of $30 million (of which $10 million are due for payment on 30 June 2012). Find the amount that should be classified as non-current on the company's balance sheet as at 31 December 2011.

Solution

- Long-term lease payable amounts to $9 million ($10 million minus $1 million which is the current portion).
- Long-term net pension liability is $18 million ($20 million minus $2 million).
- Bonds payable of $20 million ($30 million minus $10 million).

Hence, total non-current liabilities that should appear on Company's A balance sheet as at 31 December 2011 should be $47 million ($9 million plus $18 million plus $20 million)

BONDS PAYABLE

Bonds payable are liabilities which represent debt raised by a company from external investors which it vows to pay back in a specific time together with periodic interest payments over the life of the bond.

The time span in which a company has to pay back the principal plus interest is called the maturity of the bond. The periodic interest payments are called coupon payments and the interest rate specified in the contract is called coupon rate.

Bonds payable are governed by a contract called the bond indenture which specifies the terms of the bond such as maturity, repayment schedule, etc. and specifies any covenants. Positive covenants are certain obligations which the company has to fulfil during the term of bond, for example a bond indenture may require a company to maintain a times interest earned ratio of at least 3. Negative covenants are restrictions on the company; for example, a bond indenture may require a company not to have a dividend payout ratio in excess of 40%.

Example

Company B issued 100,000, $100 face value bonds carrying a coupon rate of 8% payable semi-annually. The bonds were issued on 1 January 2000 and are expected to mature in 20 years. Calculate the periodic interest payments.

Solution

The periodic interest payments equal the face value multiplied by the coupon rate applicable. In this scenario annual coupon rate is 8% but the bond will pay two payments each year so each periodic payment is 8%/2*$100*100,000 = $400,000

ISSUANCE OF BONDS PAYABLE AT PAR

When the coupon rate (i.e. the interest rate stated on the bond) is equal to the market interest rate, a company will be able to sell the bond to investors at its face value. Face value of a bond payable is the value which the company vows to pay back to the investors at maturity.

Example

Company F has issued 100 bonds of $1,000 face value on 1 January 2012. These bonds have a maturity of 5 years and carry a stated interest rate of 8% to be paid annually. The market interest rate at the time of issue was exactly 8%.

ACCOUNTING TREATMENT OF ISSUANCE AT PAR

Since there is no difference between the contractual interest rate on the bond and the interest rate prevalent in the market the bonds will be issued at par. When the bonds are issued, Company F will pass the following journal entry:

Cash	100,000	
Bonds Payable		100,000

INTEREST EXPENSE ON BONDS ISSUED AT PAR

The company's interest expense for the year ended 31 December 2012 will equal $8,000 which is the product of stated interest rate of 8% and the face value of the bonds of $100,000. Company F will record this interest expense as follows:

Interest Expense	8,000	
Cash		8,000

RETIREMENT OF BONDS ISSUED AT PAR

After 5 years Company F will repay the bonds at their face value and record the event as follows:

Bonds Payable	100,000	
Cash		100,000

ISSUANCE OF BONDS PAYABLE AT PREMIUM

When the stated interest rate on a bond is higher than the prevailing market price a company is able to sell its bonds for more than their par value. Investors consider the bond to be worth more than its par because it is offering a rate of return that is higher than the market rate of return.

Example

Company P has printed 100,000 bonds of face value of $100 each, carrying a stated interest rate of 10% and maturing in five year. When the company is ready to sell the bonds on 1 January 2013 the market rate is 8%. Since the stated interest rate is higher than the market interest rate the bonds will be issued at a premium to the par value which means the price will be higher than the par value.

The price would be $108 calculated as follows:

$$\text{Price of Bond} = 10\% \times \$100 \times \frac{1 - (1 + 8\%)^{-5}}{8\%} + \frac{\$100}{(1 + 8\%)^5} = \$108$$

ACCOUNTING TREATMENT FOR ISSUANCE OF BONDS AT PREMIUM

Company P will record this issue of bonds at a price higher than their par value using the following journal entry:

Cash	108,000	
Bonds Payable		100,000
Premium on Bonds Payable		8,000

The premium on bonds payable is added to the face value of bonds payable on the balance sheet and increases the carrying amount of the bonds.

INTEREST EXPENSE ON BONDS ISSUED AT PREMIUM

The interest expense recognized on bonds issued at premium to par is the difference between the interest paid or payable of $10,000 based on the stated interest rate of 10% (calculated as the product of 10% and the face value of $100,000) and the annual amortization of premium on bonds payable. If the premium is amortized based on a straight line method the premium of $8,000 would be written off over the 5 years of the bonds payable. Amortization of bond premium for the year would be $1,600. Company P would record the annual interest expense as follows:

Interest Expense	8,400	
Amortization of Premium	1,600	
Interest Payable/Cash		10,000

The amortization of premium on bonds reduces the carrying amount of bonds such that at the maturity the carrying amount of bonds payable approaches their face value.

RETIREMENT OF BONDS ISSUED AT PREMIUM

At maturity the carrying amount of bonds payable issued at premium approaches their face value and the bond is redeemed by paying back the principal to bondholders. Company P would record the event as follows:

	100,000	
Cash		100,000

ISSUANCE OF BONDS PAYABLE AT DISCOUNT

A bond is issued at discount when it is sold for less than its par value. When the interest rate stated on a bond is lower than the market interest rate the investor the investor consider the bond to be overvalued because it is offering a less than market return. In order to induce the investors to buy the bond the issuer is forced to reduce the price of the bond.

Example

Company D has printed 1,000 bonds of $100 par value having a maturity of 5 years and annual coupon of $8 per year. When it was finally ready to issue the bond on 1 July 2012 the interest rate prevailing in the market has soared to 10%.

ACCOUNTING TREATMENT FOR ISSUANCE AT DISCOUNT

Inventors would not be willing to buy a bond for $100 because it is overvalued at 8%. The correct value keeping in view the market interest rate of 10% is $92.42 calculated as follows:

$$\text{Price of Bond} = 8\% \times \$100 \times \frac{1 - (1 + 10\%)^{-5}}{10\%} + \frac{\$100}{(1 + 10\%)^{5}} = \$92.42$$

Company D would be able to raise only $92,420 from the bond with face value of $100,000. It has issued them at a discount of $7,580 ($100,000 minus the proceeds of $92,420). Company D will record the issuance by the following journal entry

Cash	92,420	
Discount on Bonds Payable	7,580	
Bonds Payable		100,000

Bonds payable is reported on the balance sheet net of the discount i.e. 92,420 ($100,000 face value less discount of $7,580).

RECOGNITION OF INTEREST ON BONDS ISSUED AT DISCOUNT

Interest expense in case of bonds issued at discount has two components: one related to the payment of interest based on the coupon rate and second relates to amortization of discount. Discount is amortized using either straight line method or the effective interest method. In case of Company D interest paid in cash equals $8,000 ($100,000 multiplied by the stated coupon rate of 8%). Assuming straight line amortization the yearly amortization expense should be $1,516. Total interest expense is hence $9,516 which is recorded as follows:

Interest Expense	9,516	
Interest Payable		8,000
Discount on Bonds Payable		1,516

Amortization of discount reduces the balance in the contra account to bonds payable and results in an increase in carrying amount of bonds payable. Amortization reduces the balance in discount on bonds payable account such that at the maturity the bonds payable's carrying amount is equal to its face value.

RETIREMENT OF BONDS ISSUED AT DISCOUNT

At maturity the bonds' carrying amount is equal to their face value. Company D would pay off the face value and record the event as follows:

| Bonds Payable | 100,000 | |
| Cash | | 100,000 |

AMORTIZATION OF BOND DISCOUNT: EFFECTIVE INTEREST METHOD

Under effective interest method of amortization of bond discount, the bond discount amortized each year is equal to the difference between the interest expense based on the product of market interest rate and the carrying amount of the bond and the interest payable based on the product of the stated coupon rate and face value.

Illustration

Company DS intended to issue a bond with face value of $100,000 having a maturity of 5 years and annual coupon of 8%. At the time of issue however, the market interest rate rose to 10% and the bond could fetch a price of $92,420 only.

For the first year, the interest expense is based on the market interest rate of 10% and the carrying amount of the bond of $92,420 and it equals $9,242. Interest paid or payable on the other hand is based on the stated interest rate of 8% and the face value of $100,000 and it equals $8,000. The amortization of bond discount for the first year is simply the difference between these two figures and it equals $1,242. Company SD would record the amortization and interest expense using the following journal entry:

Interest expense	9,242	
Interest payable		8,000
Bond discount		1,242

In year 2 the carrying amount would be $93,662 ($92,420 plus the amortized bond discount of $1,242). This would lead to interest expense of $9,366. Since interest paid or payable would be the same i.e. $8,000 this would lead to a higher figure for bond discount amortized during the period. Company SD would require the following journal entry:

Interest expense	9,336	
Interest payable		8,000
Bond discount		1,336

We notice that under the effective interest method the amount of bond discount amortized increases over the life of the bond.

Effective interest method is the preferred method for bond discount amortization as compared to straight line method.

PREPARING A BOND AMORTIZATION SCHEDULE

Bond amortization schedule is a table showing periodic interest expense, interest payment and amortization of discount or premium.

EFFECTIVE RATE METHOD OF BOND AMORTIZATION

Following are the steps in preparing a bond amortization schedule prepared under effective rate method of bond amortization:
- Find the opening carrying amount of the bond payable by discounting the bond's cash flows at the market interest rate (also known as the effective rate of interest);
- Calculate interest payment for the period by multiplying the par value of the bond with the stated interest rate for the period.
- Calculate interest expense for the period by multiplying the opening carrying amount with the effective rate of interest for the period;
- Find the amortization of discount or premium for the period as the difference between the interest expense and the interest payment.
- Find the closing carrying amount of the bond payable. In case of amortization of discount, add the amortization for the period to the opening carrying amount of the bond. In case of amortization of premium, subtract the amortization for the period from the opening carrying amount of the bond.

STRAIGHT-LINE METHOD OF BOND AMORTIZATION

Following are the steps in preparing a bond amortization schedule prepared under straight-line method of bond amortization:
- Find the opening carrying amount of the bond payable (the same as in effective rate of interest method;
- Find the amortization of discount or premium for the period by dividing the total discount or premium by the number of periods.
- Calculate interest payment for the period by multiplying the par value of the bond with the stated interest rate for the period.
- Calculate interest expense for the period. In case of amortization of discount, find the interest expense for the period by adding the amortization to the interest payment. In case of amortization of premium, find the interest expense for the period by subtracting the amortization from the interest payment for the period.;
- Find the closing carrying amount of the bond payable (in the same way as in effective rate of amortization method).

AMORTIZATION OF BOND DISCOUNT: STRAIGHT LINE METHOD

When the coupon rate on a bond is lower than the interest rate prevailing in the market the bond is issued at a discount to par value. Alternatively, if the coupon rate is higher than the market interest rate the bond is issued at a premium to its par value. In both cases the carrying value of the bond is different from its face value. In case of issue at a discounted issue, the carrying amount equals face value minus the discount on bond; and in case of a premium issue, the carrying amount equals face value plus the amount of premium.

In both cases the interest paid or payable is based on the coupon rate which is the stated rate of the bond. However, the interest expense reported on the income statement is higher when the bond is issued at a discount to the par value by the amount of periodic amortization of bond discount. There are two methods for amortization of bond discount: the straight line method and the effective interest rate.

STRAIGHT LINE METHOD

Under the straight line method of amortization of bond discount, the bond discount is written off in equal amounts over the life of the bond.

Example

Company DS intended to issue a bond with face value of $100,000 having a maturity of 5 years and annual coupon of 8%. At the time of issue however, the market interest rate rose to 10% and the bond could fetch a price of $92,420 only.

The difference of $7,580 between the face value of bond of $100,000 and the proceeds of $92,420 represent the discount on bond. Since the bond has a life of 5 years, the annual amortization of bond discount would equal $1,516 ($7,580 divided by 5). At the end of first year if interest payable is $8,000 Company DS would record its interest expense using the following journal entry:

Interest Expense	9,516	
Interest Payable		8,000
Bond Discount		1,516

Under straight line method the periodic interest expense, interest payable and amortization of bond discount does not vary over the periods.

GAIN OR LOSS ON EARLY RETIREMENT OF BONDS

A bond is said to be retired early when it is retired at any time before its maturity date. Accounting for bonds retired at maturity is straight forward: the company pays out cash and removes the bond payable from its balance sheet. However, when a bond is retired before maturity a gain or loss may arise. If the price paid to retire the bonds is greater the carrying amount of bonds the company needs to record a loss on retirement. On the other hand if the price paid is less than the carrying amount of the bonds at retirement the company records a gain on retirement of bonds.

Example: loss on retirement of bonds

Company L had issued $100,000 worth of bonds 2 years ago at a discount of $5,000. The current balance in the discount on bonds payable account is $4,000. The company intends to redeem the bonds for $98,000.

Carrying amount of a bond payable equals the face value of the bond less any discount or plus any premium. In this scenario the face value is $100,000 and the outstanding balance of discount on bonds payable is $4,000 which gives us a carrying amount of $96,000. Since the cash paid to redeem the bonds is $98,000 which exceeds the carrying amount of $96,000 by $2,000 the company needs to record loss of retirement of bonds of $2,000 as follows:

Bonds payable	100,000	
Loss on retirement of bonds	2,000	
Cash		98,000
Discount of bonds		4,000

Example: gain on retirement of bonds

Company G had issued $100,000 worth of bonds 2 years ago at a premium of $6,000. The current balance in the discount on bonds payable account is $5,000. The company intends to redeem the bonds for $102,000.

Carrying amount of a bond payable equals the face value of the bond less any discount or plus any premium. In this scenario the face value is $100,000 and the outstanding balance of premium on bonds payable is $5,000 which gives us a carrying amount of $105,000 ($100,000 plus $5,000). The cash paid to redeem the bonds is $102,000 which is lower than the carrying amount of $105,000. Company G should record a gain on early retirement of bonds of $3,000 because it was able to settle a liability for less than its carrying amount.

Bonds payable	100,000	
Premium on bonds	5,000	
Cash		102,000
Gain on retirement of bonds		3,000

CHAPTER FOUR
BREAK EVEN ANALYSIS

OVER VIEW

Break even analysis is the relationship between cost volume and profits at various levels of activity, with emphasis being placed on the breakeven point. The breakeven point is where the business neither receives a profit nor a loss; this is when total money received from sales is equal to total money spent to produce the items for sale.

USES OF A BREAK EVEN ANALYSIS

Break even analysis enables a business organization to:
1. Measure profit and loss at different levels of production and sales.
2. To predict the effect of changes in price of sales.
3. To analysis the relationship between fixed cost and variable cost.
4. To predict the effect on profitability if changes in cost and efficiency.

Even though break even has these advantages or uses, there are also several demerits of breakeven analysis.

DISADVANTAGES OF BREAKEVEN ANALYSIS
1. Assumes that sales prices are constant at all levels of output.
2. Assumes production and sales are the same.
3. Break even charts may be time consuming to prepare.
4. It can only apply to a single product or single mix of products.

Breakeven Chart

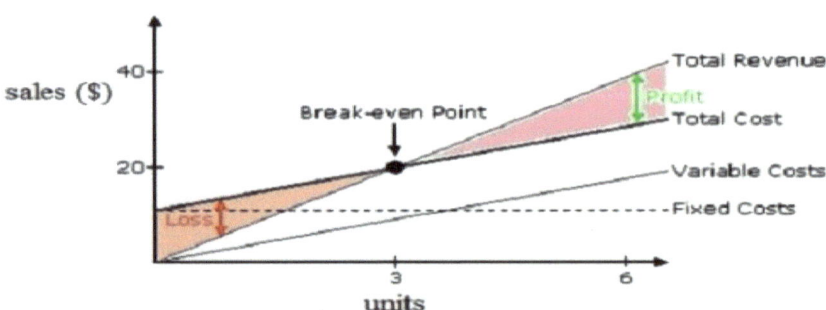

BREAK EVEN FORMULAS

BREAKEVEN POINT

There are two ways of calculating the breakeven point, in units and in sales revenue. The first way is by dividing fixed cost by contribution per unit this gives the result in units or by dividing fixed cost by c/s ratio which gives the sales revenue. The c/s ratio is the contribution to sales ratio this is given by dividing contribution per unit by selling price per unit.

Example of Breakeven point

ABC Ltd expects to sell 10000 units at $10 each. The variable cost per unit is $5 and the fixed cost is $15000 per annum. Calculate the breakeven point in units and in sale revenue. To calculate the BEP in units you would use the formula fixed cost divided by contribution per unit. Therefore you would divide $15000 by contribution which is selling price $10 minus variable cost per unit $5. $15000 divided by $5. The final answer is 3000 units In terms of sales revenue you would divide the fixed cost by the c/s ratio. $15000 divided by (contribution divided by selling price per unit) . $15000 divided by ($5 divided by $10).$15000 divided by 0.5. The final answer is $30000. And we know this is the correct answer because when we multiply the breakeven point in units by the selling price we get the same answer.

CONSTRUCTION

In the linear Cost-Volume-Profit Analysis model (where marginal costs and marginal revenues are constant, among other assumptions), the **break-even point (BEP)** (in terms of Unit Sales (X)) can be directly computed in terms of Total Revenue (TR) and Total Costs (TC) as:

$$\mathrm{TR} = \mathrm{TC}$$
$$\mathrm{P} \times \mathrm{X} = \mathrm{TFC} + \mathrm{V} \times \mathrm{X}$$
$$\mathrm{P} \times \mathrm{X} - \mathrm{V} \times \mathrm{X} = \mathrm{TFC}$$
$$(\mathrm{P} - \mathrm{V}) \times \mathrm{X} = \mathrm{TFC}$$
$$\mathrm{X} = \frac{\mathrm{TFC}}{\mathrm{P} - \mathrm{V}}$$

Where:
- TFC is Total Fixed Costs,
- P is Unit Sale Price, and
- V is Unit Variable Cost.

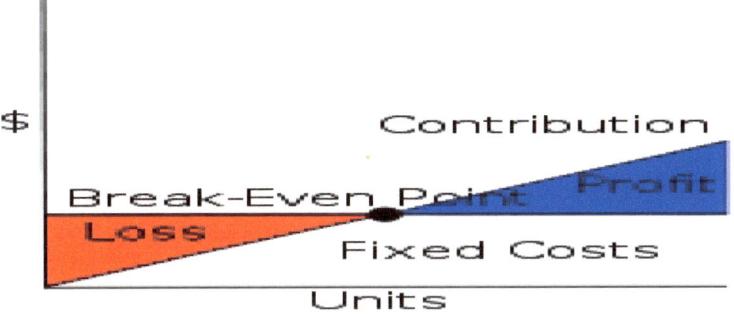

The Break-Even Point can alternatively be computed as the point where Contribution equals Fixed Costs.

The quantity, $(\mathrm{P} - \mathrm{V})$, is of interest in its own right, and is called the Unit Contribution Margin (C): it is the marginal profit per unit, or alternatively the portion of each sale that contributes to Fixed Costs. Thus the break-even point can be more simply computed as the point where Total Contribution = Total Fixed Cost:

$$\text{Total Contribution} = \text{Total Fixed Costs}$$
$$\text{Unit Contribution} \times \text{Number of Units} = \text{Total Fixed Costs}$$
$$\text{Number of Units} = \frac{\text{Total Fixed Costs}}{\text{Unit Contribution}}$$

To calculate the break-even point in terms of revenue (a.k.a. currency units, a.k.a. sales proceeds) instead of Unit Sales (X), the above calculation can be multiplied by Price, or, equivalently, the Contribution Margin Ratio (Unit Contribution Margin over Price) can be calculated:

$$\text{Break-even(in Sales)} = \frac{\text{Fixed Costs}}{\text{C/P}}.$$

R=C,

Where R is revenue generated, C is cost incurred
i.e. Fixed costs + Variable Costs or Q * P (Price per unit) = TFC + Q * VC (Price per unit),
Q * P - Q * VC = TFC,
Q * (P - VC) = TFC, or,
Break Even Analysis Q = TFC/c/s ratio=Break Even

MARGIN OF SAFETY
Margin of safety represents the strength of the business. It enables a business to know what the exact amount it has gained or lost is and whether they are over or below the break-even point.
Margin of safety = (current output - breakeven output)
Margin of safety% = (current output - breakeven output)/current output × 100
When dealing with budgets you would instead replace "Current output" with "Budgeted output."
If P/V ratio is given then profit/PV ratio

BREAK-EVEN ANALYSIS
By inserting different prices into the formula, you will obtain a number of break-even points, one for each possible price charged. If the firm changes the selling price for its product, from $2 to $2.30, in the example above, then it would have to sell only 1000/(2.3 - 0.6)= 589 units to break even, rather than 715.

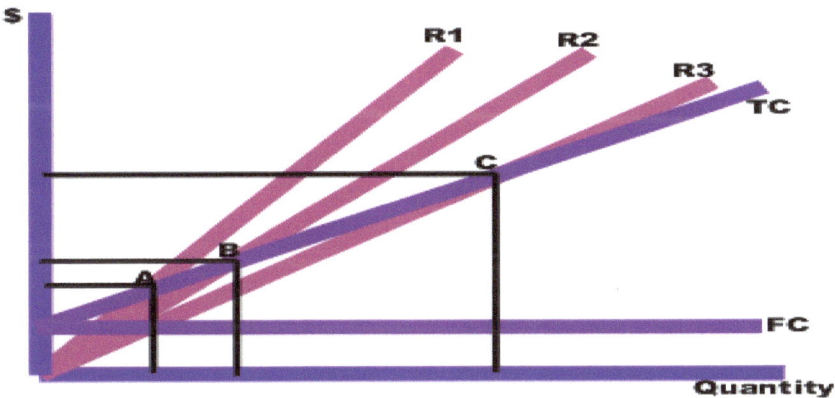

To make the results clearer, they can be graphed. To do this, you draw the total cost curve (TC in the diagram) which shows the total cost associated with each possible level of output, the fixed cost curve (FC) which shows the costs that do not vary with output level, and finally the various total revenue lines (R1, R2, and R3) which show the total amount of revenue received at each output level, given the price you will be charging.

The break-even points (A,B,C) are the points of intersection between the total cost curve (TC) and a total revenue curve (R1, R2, or R3). The break-even quantity at each selling price can be read off the horizontal axis and the break-even price at each selling price can be read off the vertical axis. The total cost, total revenue, and fixed cost curves can each be constructed with simple formula. For example, the total revenue curve is simply the product of selling price times quantity for each output quantity. The data used in this formula come either from accounting records or from various estimation techniques such as regression analysis.

LIMITATIONS

- Break-even analysis is only a supply-side (i.e., costs only) analysis, as it tells you nothing about what sales are actually likely to be for the product at these various prices.
- It assumes that fixed costs (FC) are constant. Although this is true in the short run, an increase in the scale of production is likely to cause fixed costs to rise.
- It assumes average variable costs are constant per unit of output, at least in the range of likely quantities of sales. (i.e., linearity).
- It assumes that the quantity of goods produced is equal to the quantity of goods sold (i.e., there is no change in the quantity of goods held in inventory at the beginning of the period and the quantity of goods held in inventory at the end of the period).
- In multi-product companies, it assumes that the relative proportions of each product sold and produced are constant (i.e., the sales mix is constant).

REFERENCE

Garrison, R. H., P. E. Noreen, 'Managerial Accounting', Irwin McGraw Hill, 1999

Horngren, C. T. and G. Foster, 'Cost Accounting, A Managerial Emphasis', Prentice-Hall, Inc. 1987

Johnson, H. T. and R. S. Kaplan, 'Relevance Lost: The Rise and Fall of Management Accounting', Harvard Business School Press, 1987.

Kaplan, R.S. and A. A. Atkinson, 'Advanced Management Accounting', Prentice-Hall International Inc. 1989

Kaplan, R. S., D. P. Norton, 'The Balanced Scorecard - Measures that Drive Performance', Harvard Business Review, January - February 1992.

Kaplan, R. S., D. P. Norton, 'The Strategy Focused Organization', 2001, Harvard Business School Publishing Corporation

Solomons, D., 'Historical Development of Costing', Studies in Costing, Sweet & Maxwell, 1952, pp. 1-51.